C000258470

THE SWALLOW

HAMLYN SPECIES GUIDES

THE SWALLOW

Angela Turner

HAMLYN

COVER ILLUSTRATION *Adult male swallow displaying in flight.*

First published in 1994 by Hamlyn Limited,
an imprint of Reed Consumer Books Ltd
Michelin House, 81 Fulham Road, London SW3 6RB
and Auckland, Melbourne, Singapore and Toronto

Copyright © Reed International Books Limited 1994

Text copyright © Angela Turner 1994
Colour illustrations copyright © Hilary Burn 1994
Black and white illustrations copyright © Norman Arlott 1994
Map copyright © Reed International Books Limited 1994

The photographs are copyright and are reproduced by permission of the following:
p 6 © K. Taylor/Bruce Coleman Ltd; p 10 © R. Glover/Aquila; p 15, 46, 63, 79 ©
R. Tidman; p 38 © E. K. Thompson/Aquila; p 47 © R. Glover/Bruce Coleman Ltd;
p 51 © D. Green/Bruce Coleman Ltd; p 59, 87, 90 © A. Cardwell/Aquila; p 70 ©
R. P. Carr/Bruce Coleman Ltd; p. 75 © M. Rains; p 83 © F. Marquez/Bruce Coleman Ltd;
p 86 © M. C. Wilkes/Aquila; p 103 © D. Canning/Nature Photographers Ltd; p 114 ©
P. Sterry/Nature Photographers Ltd; p 119 © K. Carlson/Nature Photographers Ltd.

ISBN 0 600 57979 4

All rights reserved. Apart from any fair dealing for the purpose of private study, research,
criticism or review, as permitted under the Copyright Designs and Patents Act, 1988,
no part of this publication may be reproduced, stored in a retrieval system, or transmitted
in any form or by any means, electronic, electrical, chemical, mechanical, optical,
photocopying, recording, or otherwise, without prior written permission. All enquiries
should be addressed to the Publishers.

A CIP catalogue record for this book is available from the British Library

Page design by Jessica Caws
Maps by Louise Griffiths
Printed in Hong Kong

CONTENTS

Series Editor's Foreword

Widely renowned in the northern hemisphere as a herald of spring, the Swallow is a favourite bird of many people in many countries. It is equally familiar to the inhabitants in its wintering quarters in Africa, South America and southern Asia, where some winter roosts can number hundreds of thousands of individuals.

Despite the high esteem in which this elegant bird is held, however, there are some aspects of its life which come as a surprise. Promiscuity is not uncommon, and cuckoldry is rife among males, which also frequently kill young in other nests, while females often deposit eggs in other Swallows' nests, leaving the hard work of rearing the chicks to the unwitting foster parents.

There are, of course, good reasons for these apparently 'antisocial' habits, and these are explained in the following pages. The reason why males have such long tails, which vary in length from one individual to the next, is something few birdwatchers ever wonder about, yet tail length is of supreme importance within the context of mate-selection: females choose those males with the longest tail-streamers, and why they do so is again explained in simple terms in this book.

Angela Turner has studied Swallows extensively for many years, and in her highly readable text, she recounts the life of this strikingly handsome bird in the most fascinating detail and corrects some of the misconceptions about it. Nobody now believes that Swallows hibernate in mud at the bottom of ponds and rivers, but only a couple of centuries ago, it was almost heretical to suggest otherwise. The fact that millions of these small insect-eating birds undertake twice yearly a hazardous migration across the Sahara, where many perish in the extreme conditions, is surely, however, an equally if not more wondrous feat.

The Swallow has always featured prominently in mythology and legend. It has been seen as a bringer both of good luck and of bad luck, it has been credited with having the most amazing magical and medicinal properties, and it has been regarded almost with reverence in some religions. For me and, I suspect, for many others, the Swallow conjures up pictures of a graceful and most welcome bird which, with its pleasant twittering song and its apparent lack of fear of humans, adds so much charm to our farmyards in spring and summer. The next time I watch nesting Swallows, however, I shall look more closely at the length of the male's tail streamers!

David A Christie

A male Swallow bringing food in its throat to the nest.

Acknowledgements

I am grateful to Melanie Heath for comments and permission to use data from the BirdLife International/European Bird Census Council European Bird Database and *Birds in Europe: Their Conservation Status* prior to publication; to David Gibbons for a preview of the new *Atlas* data on Swallows; to Bruce Peterjohn for the North American Breeding Bird Survey trend estimates for Barn Swallows; and to Linda Birch at the Edward Grey Institute for library facilities. Since I started my studies of Swallows at Stirling and while writing this book, many people have helped me by providing stimulating discussion, comments on chapters, information, translations, previews of papers, or recent reprints: I thank particularly David Bryant, Florentino de Lope, Jan Allex de Roos, Gareth Jones, Karl-Heinz Loske, Anders Pape Møller, Sally Ward and David Waugh. I also thank the many farmers and landowners who gave me permission to wander over their land and study their Swallows and David Christie, Jo Hemmings and Samantha Ward-Dutton for their vital work on the final stages of this book.

1

AN INTRODUCTION
TO SWALLOWS

*'A Swallow
Has slipped through a fracture in the snow-sheet
Which is still our sky'*
Ted Hughes

In late April in Scotland, when the winter snow is melting and rain is pattering on the surface of lochs and rivers, newly arrived, hungry migrants come to feed on the swarming insects dancing over the water. A dozen small, streamlined birds may be seen zig–zagging, taking their fill of tiny flies. The majority will be Sand Martins, brown and white darts, expert aerial hunters of insect life. Among them, a larger bird may stand out. Its back, a shiny metallic blue, contrasts strongly with its creamy-white underparts and red forehead and throat, and long tail-streamers extend gracefully behind it as it swoops after insect prey: the first Swallow of the year, promising that summer is not far away.

Skimming low over our fields and lakes in pursuit of insects, the Swallow is a familiar and welcome sight. Its confiding nature and its habit of building a nest so close to our own homes endear it to many people. Those fortunate enough to be host to a pair eagerly await the return of 'their' Swallows each spring. The Swallow's departure in autumn, in contrast, is a sad event, a reminder of the storms and frost to come.

There are 75 species of swallows in the world, of which only three breed in Britain: the Sand Martin, the House Martin and the Swallow. This book is a portrait of the most widespread and one of the best-known species, and the one that has given its name to this family of aerial-hunting birds. The English name 'swallow' is a very old one. It probably comes from the Old English root verb *'swel'* meaning to swirl, a reference to the bird's swooping flight. The Anglo–Saxon was *Swealwe* and in Old Saxon the name was *Swala*. The name is similar elsewhere in Europe, the Old High German version being *Swalwa* and the Old Norse *Svala*. The scientific name of our Swallow is *Hirundo rustica*. *Hirundo* is the Latin for a swallow and *rustica* means rural or rustic. The Greeks used the name *Chelidon*, and this is commemorated in anagrammatic form in the scientific name for the House Martin, *Delichon urbica* – the town swallow. The common names, old and modern, in various countries often refer to the nesting sites of the bird: House or Chimney Swallow in Britain, Barn Swallow in North America, *Rauchschwalbe* or *Feuerschwalbe* in Germany, *Hirondelle de Cheminée* or *Hirondelle Domestique* in France, *Golondrina de Chimenea* in Spain.

This adult Swallow clearly shows the long outer tail streamers and white spots in the tail.

The present English name, however, does not distinguish the Swallow from all the other swallows in the world, so the name Barn Swallow has been suggested. It is already used in North America and neatly describes the bird's characteristic nest site. The species is being referred to by an increasing number of British birdwatchers as Barn Swallow.

By whatever name it is known, the Swallow is a beautiful and fascinating bird just to watch and admire. Because of its long association with humans, it has become a popular figure in mythology, folklore and superstition, and recently it has also been the subject of a great deal of scientific research. I spent several years studying the feeding behaviour of Swallows on farms around Stirling in Central Scotland, and many other studies have investigated other aspects of their biology and behaviour, both in Europe and in North America. In this account, I concentrate on the Swallow in Europe, and particularly in Britain, but I include information on its North American population where this is of particular interest.

The other British aerial feeding birds: House Martin, Sand Martin and Swift.

Hilary Burn

The swallow family

Members of the swallow family are collectively known as hirundines (the family Hirundinidae), a group of the passerines or songbirds. It includes birds known as martins, as well as swallows, but these two names refer essentially to the same sorts of birds, although 'martin' often refers to a bird with a square tail and 'swallow' to one with a forked tail. The names are sometimes used interchangeably, however: thus the Sand Martin we know in Britain is called a Bank Swallow in North America, while an old British name for the House Martin is 'Window Swallow'.

The hirundine family contains two types (or subfamilies) of swallow: the Pseudochelidoninae, or river martins, and the Hirundininae. The two species of river martins are stocky birds, intermediate between swallows and other songbirds: the African River Martin is found only in Central Africa, and the White-eyed River Martin is known to winter in Thailand, (although where it breeds is a mystery). The remaining hirundines, including our British Swallow, form a well-defined group, and its members are very similar in many respects.

Internally, their syrinx (a bird's vocal apparatus, situated at the base of the neck) is distinctive because it has more or less complete rings of cartilage around the bronchi, whereas other passerines have half-rings with just a membrane across the inner face. Externally, too, the family is distinctive. Swallows and martins are typically streamlined, with long wings, a slender body and short neck, and a small, broad beak. Their shape is constrained by the way they live. They all feed on the wing, chasing insects in flight, so they are designed for skilful aerobatic manoeuvring. Some of the species have a forked tail, with elongated outer feathers, which helps them to check in flight and to turn quickly when pursuing their prey. Those with squarer tails, such as the Sand Martin, are less manoeuvrable but still impressively aerobatic.

The flattened beak and strong jaw muscles of hirundines allow them to open their mouths wide and to snap at insects flying past. Bristles around the gape are also an aid to capturing prey, as are the loral feathers, in front of the eye, which are directed forward to act as a lens shade. Unlike many birds, which have monocular vision, hirundines have two light sensitive areas (the fovea) in their eyes, placed to provide some binocular vision, which is important for judging the distance of prey.

Swallows and martins have short legs, and their feet are rather small and weak because they do little walking. On the ground they usually do no more than shuffle or, at best, run a short distance. The legs and feet are more useful for perching or for clinging to cliff faces. The front toes are more or less united at the base, the legs are ridged at the rear, and the legs and feet are sometimes partly or fully feathered.

As well as their prowess in the air, swallows and martins are well known for their building skills. Although many species, such as the Tree Swallow and Purple Martin in the New World, just make do with a simple tangle of twigs and grass in a hole in a bank, cliff or tree, some, such as the Sand Martin, excavate their own burrows and others, such as the

Swallow, construct sturdy bowls of mud. Both the open mud nests of Swallows and the enclosed nests of House Martins are familiar structures plastered on to walls or on the beams inside buildings.

The members of the Hirundine family range in size from the diminutive White-thighed Swallow of South America, which is 12 cm (4¾ in) long and weighs 9.5 g, to the large Purple Martin of North America, 19 cm (7½ in) long and weighing in at a relatively hefty 48 – 64 g.

Many species are a striking metallic blue or green on the head, back and wings, often with contrasting white, buff or rufous underparts and similar colouring on the face or rump or both. Some species also sport a breast-band. Many have white patches in the tail or on the wings. The male and female are usually similar, although, in species with elongated tails, the males have longer outer tail feathers (streamers) than the females.

Swallows build their nests from mud and dry grass.

The genus *Hirundo*, to which our Swallow belongs, is also widely distributed throughout the Americas, Europe, Africa, Asia and Australasia. It comprises 34 species, all the swallows and martins that build mud nests, apart from the three species of house martins, which are, however, very closely related to them. This genus includes several well-defined groups: crag martins, barn swallows, wire-tailed swallows, pearl-breasted swallows, mosque and red-rumped swallows, blue and striped swallows, and cliff swallows. Many of the species have a metallic plumage with a forked tail, and contrasting red forehead, throat or rump. The underparts vary from creamy-white to rufous, sometimes streaked and sometimes with a chest-band, and the tail feathers often bear white patches.

The Swallow itself is part of a closely related group of species which all look very similar but which occur in largely separate parts of the world: the Red-chested Swallow of Africa in the northern tropics; the Angolan

Swallow of Equatorial Africa; the White-throated Swallow of Southern Africa; the Ethiopian Swallow of Central Africa; the Pacific Swallow of India, south-east Asia and the islands of the Pacific; and the Welcome Swallow of Australasia.

Swallows and martins form such a distinctive group that their relationship with other birds was for many years obscure. They do not look like members of other groups apart from the swifts, and early naturalists classified these birds together. All manner of swallows, martins and swifts were lumped into the single genus *Hirundo*. Their similarities in shape, however, stem from their similarities in lifestyle. Because swallows, martins and swifts spend so much time on the wing, feeding on insects in flight, they all need to be streamlined with long wings. It was only towards the end of the nineteenth century, when R. B. Sharpe and C. W. Wyatt wrote the first monograph on the hirundines, that swallows and martins were recognized as a distinct family within the order Passeriformes, quite unrelated to the swifts, which are in a separate order, Apodiformes. Taxonomists have at various times considered swallows and martins to be closely related to flycatchers, larks, pipits and wagtails, cuckoo-shrikes, drongos, white-eyes, waxwings, starlings or Old World warblers – in other words, they did not really know. Recent analysis of their DNA has now placed them in a group of birds containing the nuthatches, treecreepers and wrens, titmice, long-tailed tits, kinglets, bulbuls, African warblers, white-eyes, and Old World warblers and babblers. Swallows and martins are thought to have diverged from the rest of this group about 50 million years ago and now look very different from them.

The Swallow

Its aerial habits, shiny blue back contrasting with creamy underparts, and red throat and forehead make the Swallow easy to identify. In flight, the Swallow can appear quite large, but the long wings and elongated tail are deceptive. It is only a small, light-weight bird, just 18 cm (7 in) long, of which 3 – 8 cm comprise the tail streamers, and, on the breeding grounds, it usually weighs 16 – 23 g (averaging 19 g).

The male Swallow has a glossy metallic blue-black head and back, and a distinctive band of the same hue running across his chest. There are sometimes a few chestnut or buff feathers in the centre of the band but they do not interrupt it. Above the band, the throat, chin and forehead are a striking chestnut-red. The brilliance of the back is offset by the pale belly, the male's underparts from chest to vent and including the underwing-coverts and undertail-coverts being generally a shade of buff, although they vary from off-white to almost rufous, with the undertail-coverts somewhat darker than the rest of the belly. The wings are black with a steel-green or blue-green gloss; there are ten primaries, but, as in all species of swallows, the outermost is extremely reduced. The tail is also black or brownish-black with a blue or blue-green gloss; the feathers, apart from the central pair,

Juvenile Swallows are duller than the adults and have shorter tails.

bear white patches near the tip, but these are often not visible when the bird is perching, unless he spreads his tail. The outer pair of tail feathers forms long streamers, accentuating the fork of the tail. The dull black undersides of the flight feathers and tail clearly contrast with the buffy underparts when the bird is seen from below. The bill is black, sometimes with a little yellow near the gape; the legs and feet are black, sometimes with a reddish-brown tinge; and the eyes are dark brown.

Worn plumage is less glossy. The metallic sheen of the head and body is due to the glossy tips of the feathers; when these are abraded, the feathers look much duller. The bases of the feathers also often show through: white on the back and hindneck, grey on the top of the head and throat. Worn underparts look whiter or paler, often no more than a pale buff.

It is difficult to tell the male and female apart just from their appearance. The female is somewhat paler below and has a duller, rather mottled, band across the chest. The glossy, blue tips of the feathers on the upperparts and chest-band are narrower, and the grey bases of the feathers show through rather more. However, there is considerable overlap between different males and females. The female also has slightly shorter wings and a noticeably shorter tail with less elongated streamers. The male's tail is 20 per cent longer than the female's: in the European race, 87 – 132 mm versus 73 – 106 mm. The tail fork (the difference between the tips of the innermost and outermost tail feathers when the tail is folded) is usually at least 51 mm on males and less than this on females. (The reasons why males have longer tails are detailed in Chapter 5.)

In the male, the patch of white on the outer tail feather is longer (20 – 34 mm, as against 13 – 26 mm in females) and the tip of this feather is often narrower, but this is a poor criterion for sexing birds. If you see a pair of Swallows together, the female may stand out as having a shorter tail, but telling the sexes apart like this is not reliable. In the hand, one can make more precise measurements, and, in summer, the presence of a well-vascularized incubation patch indicates a female. The tail grows longer between a bird's first and second years, more so in the male than the female, while changes in subsequent years are very small. The wings also lengthen with age.

The juvenile is quite distinctive. It has dull, brownish rather than glossy blue, upperparts and pale underparts, and the tail-streamers are short. The forehead patch is paler and narrower than on the adult, and the chin and throat are also a paler buff or rufous. The chest-band is dull and mottled, the central feathers often having buff fringes. There are pale edges to the tips of the inner primaries, secondaries and tail feathers. The fork of the tail is less than 31 mm, and the outer tail feather is less than 72 mm long. The white patch on this feather is also less elongated than on adult males (length 12 – 24 mm), and the feather tip is broader. The gape is yellow and the feet sometimes have a grey tinge. Juveniles of the two sexes are very similar, though the male has a slightly blacker chest-band and a longer tail fork. After the first moult the first-year birds look the same as the adults, although some birds in their first summer may retain traces of juvenile plumage.

The coloration of Swallows varies geographically, especially in the tone of the underparts and the extent of the band across the chest. The Middle Eastern race *transitiva* has darker rufous-buff underparts and the Egyptian *savignii* is even darker, a rufous-chestnut. The Asian race *gutturalis* has pale cream or whitish underparts and only a narrow black band across the lower part of the chest. The Central Asian race *tytleri* also has only a narrow chest-band, but its underparts range from cinnamon-rufous to rufous-chestnut. The North American race *erythrogaster* has rusty-buff underparts and the band is reduced to patches on either side of the chest. The races also differ in size, the largest being *rustica* in Scandinavia, and they get smaller as one goes from the north-west to the south and east, the smallest being *gutturalis* from the south-east. Even within one race, however, one can find slight differences in coloration and size. The underparts of British *rustica* mostly vary from off-white to cream-buff, while Scandinavian and Russian *rustica* have generally whiter bellies, more like *gutturalis* in eastern Asia. Swallows in zones where two races grade into one another are particularly variable. Other races have been proposed, but are not clearly separable from those described above.

Similar species

Throughout its breeding and wintering ranges, the Swallow is very distinctive, with its combination of rufous-chestnut forehead, chin and throat, dark head and back, well-defined chest-band, pale belly and long outer tail feathers. The graceful way in which it flies, swooping after insects, is also characteristic. Three other British birds, however, look similar at first glance and they all feed on the wing.

The House Martin is perhaps the most easily confused (some people may believe they have Swallows nesting under their eaves when in fact they have House Martins). It has a blue-black head, back and wings like the Swallow, but it has purer white underparts and a conspicuous white rump; it also lacks the red forehead, chin and throat and the blue chest-band of the Swallow, has a short tail with no streamers, and its legs and feet are covered with white feathers. House Martins usually fly higher, and more slowly, than Swallows. They nest colonially on the outside of buildings, usually under eaves, building an enclosed mud nest with a small entrance at the top. Despite their differences, there have been several records of hybrids between Swallows and House Martins.

The Sand Martin is smaller than the Swallow, brown above with a brown chest-band, a white face and throat and a short, squarish tail. Its flight is more fluttery than the Swallow's. It does not nest on buildings but digs a burrow 0.6 – 1 m long into river banks or sandy cliffs, where it makes a simple nest of dry grass and feathers.

The Swift, as mentioned above, is not related to Swallows but is similar in shape. It is a large bird, uniformly dark brown except for a whitish throat patch, with sickle-shaped wings and a short fork to the tail. It nests in crevices and holes under eaves and inside roofs and is often seen dashing around the tops of houses, screaming shrilly.

Male

Adult male

Female

Adult female

Juvenile

Juvenile

On the European mainland, the only other long-tailed swallow which may cause confusion is the Red-rumped Swallow. Unlike the Swallow, however, it has a chestnut collar and rump and black undertail-coverts; it also lacks the Swallow's dark chest-band and white tail spots, and has a slower flight. Its enclosed mud nest, which has a long entrance tunnel, is attached to rock faces or buildings. Occasional aberrant Swallows or hybrids between the Swallow and the House Martin may also have a pale rump and look similar to the Red-rumped Swallow, but the two species are usually easy to distinguish. The other European swallow, the Crag Martin, looks quite different, being brown with a square tail. It is also a slow flyer, often gliding around its cliff nest sites.

In Africa, although the adult Swallow is distinctive, the juvenile, without long outer tail feathers, looks similar to the Red-chested Swallow. The latter, however, has a narrower chest-band and more white in the tail.

Male, female and juvenile plumages compared.

2

DISTRIBUTION, POPULATION AND HABITAT

'The swallow, for a moment seen,
Skims in haste the village green'
Thomas Warton

The Swallow is a phenomenally successful bird. It is one of the most widespread bird species in the world, breeding throughout most of North America, Europe and Asia, except the cold high Arctic. The race *rustica* breeds throughout Europe and Russia east to the Yenisei river. The northern part of the range extends to latitude 70°N in Norway. Pairs sometimes breed in Iceland and the Faroes, and on Malta. This race also breeds in the Middle East and in Asia as far east as western Sinkiang in China. To the south, the range extends to northernmost Africa east to Libya. In Britain the Swallow is widespread, and is absent or scarce in only a few places, notably the upland areas of north-west Scotland, the Outer Hebrides and Shetland. Since the early 1970s, however, breeding has been more regular in these latter regions.

The race *transitiva* has a restricted range in southern Turkey, the Lebanon, Syria, western Jordan and Israel, while *savignii* occurs only in Egypt throughout the Nile Delta, the Faiyum and the Suez Canal area, as far south as the Aswan High Dam, and along the north coast west to El Hammum. The race *tytleri* is the swallow of central Asia, from the Angara basin in Siberia east to the Yakutsk and the Olekma river, and south to northern Mongolia. The breeding range of *gutturalis* covers eastern Asia, and includes Japan. In the New World, *erythrogaster* breeds throughout North America: from south-eastern Alaska and much of Canada, except the far north, the range extends south through most of the United States into Mexico. Members of this American race have also bred in Argentina, which is part of the wintering range, since at least 1980.

In areas where two races meet, Swallows of one race will mate with those of the other, forming zones of hybrids intermediate between the two. The races *rustica* and *gutturalis* intergrade in the Himalayas. In the Amur territory, *gutturalis* and *tytleri* have come together relatively recently with the unwitting aid of humans. When Russian immigrants colonized the area in the seventeenth century, they constructed houses suitable for Swallows to build their nests on in an area previously lacking any suitable nesting sites; the Swallows from both east and west were able to colonize the Amur and interbred with each other, so that the population there is now intermediate between *gutturalis* and *tytleri*.

Population size and changes

The population density of Swallows varies a great deal depending on the availability of nest sites. Nests are likely to be clumped at a few sites, with large areas of unsuitable nesting habitat between them. There can be fewer than one pair per km^2 or more than thirty. In various European studies, however, densities of a few pairs per km^2 have usually been recorded: 0.5 – 34 in Britain, 5.3 – 12.4 in Denmark, 1 – 3 in Finland, 4.9 in Sweden, 6.3 – 11.4 in Poland and 1.6 – 11 in Germany.

The British Trust for Ornithology has been monitoring breeding populations and the distributions of many bird species, including Swallows, in the United Kingdom for over thirty years. This scheme, known as the Common Birds Census, reveals that Swallows are most common in Ireland and parts of eastern England and least common in northern England and Scotland. The latest estimate of the size of the breeding population in the UK is 600,000 pairs.

BirdLife International's recent review of the conservation status of European birds indicates that the Swallow's European breeding population is between 13 million and 33 million pairs, but in some areas, especially in the east of the region, the population sizes are poorly known (information from BirdLife International/European Bird Census Council European Bird Database 1993). For example, data are qualitative for Russia, which may have one million or as many as 10 million pairs, and information on the Bulgarian population of over 500,000 pairs is also sparse.

Populations of Swallows typically fluctuate in size. Subject to the vagaries of the weather, numbers can be drastically cut in one year but bounce back in subsequent years. However, there has been a widespread decline of between 20 and 50 per cent over the past twenty years in many areas of Europe, including the Czech Republic, Denmark, Estonia, Finland, France, Italy, Norway, Romania, Slovakia, Spain, Sweden, Switzerland and Britain; Germany and the Netherlands have fared particularly badly, with losses of at least half their breeding populations in this period (information from BirdLife International/European Bird Census Council European Bird Database 1993). In western Europe there are particularly large numbers in France (one million), Germany (one to two million), Portugal (one million), Spain (783,000 to 812,000) and Britain (600,000).

In Britain, the population was stable in the 1960s when the Common Birds Census began. Over the past twenty years, numbers dropped in 1974 but then recovered for a few years, until starting a steady, marked decline in the 1980s. There was a slight recovery in 1988, and the trend over the last five years (to 1992) has been an increase but the population declined significantly in 1991. The greatest decline has been in southern and eastern England, the most intensively farmed areas of the country. Since 1962, nest losses during incubation have become more frequent and nest losses during the nestling stage were very high in 1990 – 92.

21

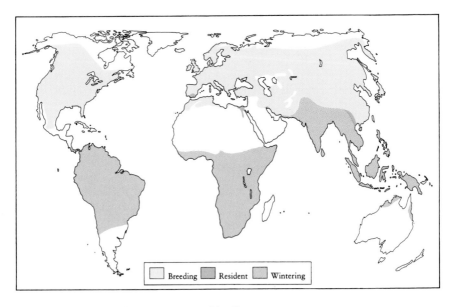

The breeding and wintering ranges of Swallows.

The range of the Swallow in Europe has remained largely the same in the last twenty years, with small contractions in Albania, Andorra, Austria, Lichtenstein, Moldova, Romania, Spain and the Ukraine (information from BirdLife International/European Bird Census Council European Bird Database 1993). In Britain, the distribution recorded in the British Trust for Ornithology's Atlas survey of 1988 – 91 has remained essentially the same since the first Atlas survey in 1968 – 72, apart from the increase in the north-west. In North Africa, the race *savignii* has expanded its range since the 1920s, when it bred only south to Luxor and east of Alexandria. The race *transitiva* also recolonized the shores of the western Galilee in the 1980s, after it disappeared in the 1950s. We do not know enough about the Asian populations to assess how they are faring.

In the New World, Swallow numbers have increased and their range has expanded since white settlers arrived. Most recently, the range has extended south towards the Gulf of Mexico in Louisiana, Mississippi and Alabama and along the Florida peninsula. Swallows were not known to breed in Florida, for example, until 1946, but the population expanded in the 1970s in particular and now they regularly breed there as far south as the Upper Keys.

When white settlers first arrived in North America, they cleared large areas of forest and established new farms, hamlets and towns, providing many more nesting sites for Swallows. A further boost to Swallow populations this century has been the building of dams and highway bridges, which have provided abundant nesting sites with little disturbance. The presence of buildings in otherwise unsuitable areas such as the tundra

22

has also allowed Swallows to expand their range. Even out-of-the-way sites such as isolated cabins in woodland clearings, boltheads on culverts in remote logging areas and fishing shacks on islands are appropriated by prospecting Swallows.

The North American Breeding Bird Survey, which was started in 1966, has shown a slight increase since then in the population in the United States but not in Canada, while between 1982 and 1991 many parts of the continent have seen small but significant declines, with an overall decrease of 2.7 per cent per year. Only a few States – Georgia, Louisiana, Mississippi and North Dakota – have had recent population increases.

Breeding habitat

Modern-day Swallows are enterprising in their use of habitats in which to breed: from the cold subarctic to the warm Mediterranean, from the wet British uplands to the dry southern steppes of Europe, high up on mountains, and along the sea coast. So long as they have a good supply of flying insects throughout the summer, a source of mud and a suitable support for their nests, Swallows can breed almost anywhere. Indeed, practically everywhere where humans have left their mark in wood, brick or stone Swallows have claimed them as their own. Farmland, villages, lake and river shorelines, roads with bridges and culverts, parks, and woodland or forest clearings are all used. All that Swallows require as a source of insects is an area with shallow water or a covering of low vegetation. So only dense woods or forests, large modern Western conurbations, deserts, and arid or rocky areas are generally unsuitable.

The range of altitudes used is also wide. Swallows breed at up to 1800 m in the Swiss Alps, up to 2000 m in central Asia and up to 3000 m in the Caucasus. At these altitudes Swallows are limited partly by the availability of water and vegetation. In Britain, they are scarcest in the uplands, perhaps because of a lack of suitable nesting sites, because of a poor food supply in the generally cool, wet climate or because of a scarcity of suitable mud for building the nests.

In Europe, Swallows are usually very much a rural bird, breeding mainly on farms and on occasions venturing into villages. This may be because they prefer to nest in quiet outhouses and barns rather than exposed on the walls of houses, or because good foraging areas are likely to be scarce in modern, large towns. In North America, Swallows are also rural but there they are more birds of highways, nesting under bridges and in culverts. Swallows do sometimes, however, nest in built-up areas. In the Yamato Basin in Japan, for example, where the Red-rumped Swallow also breeds, the Swallow is the town swallow, building its nests under eaves even along busy streets, in markets and in railway stations, and the Red-rumped is the rural swallow. In many North African and Asian towns and villages, Swallows are common breeding birds; even in large conurbations such as Cairo, they nest and feed in streets crowded with people.

The place chosen for breeding must have several features. There must be sites with plenty of insects to catch, particularly large insects such as horse-flies and bluebottles; a site with livestock present, particularly cattle, is likely to be especially well endowed in this respect. Shelterbelts, open waterbodies and other sites where insects can still be found in bad weather when they are scarce elsewhere are very important (see Chapter 3). The nest site itself needs a firm substrate to which the nest can be attached, close to an overhang or roof which provides protection from predators and the elements, and an easy entrance and exit such as an open door or empty windowframe. There must also be a supply of mud close by for building the nest, and a place near the nest for perching.

Most Swallows now breed in close association with people, nesting on or in barns, outhouses, sheds, garages, boathouses, porches and stables, or, especially in North America, on bridges, in culverts, on dams or under wharves. Pillboxes, put up along the British coast in World War II, are often used. Before the advent of centrally heated homes, the ledges of large chimney stacks used to be a popular nest site; the old British name of Chimney Swallow, and the European names such as *Rauchschwalbe* in Germany and *Hirondelle de Cheminée* in France, attest to the species' liking for such sites.

There are few present-day records of natural sites such as cliff and rock faces, caves or trees being used. In some areas, such as the Central Asian steppes, where human populations are low, Swallows still regularly use rock faces or other natural substrates, but these are considered exceptional. In the Old World, Swallows have been nesting on human artefacts for many centuries, in some areas probably for thousands of years, as literature and folklore attest, and they now rely almost totally on humans for nest sites.

In North America, the transition to artificial sites has been more recent, following colonization by Europeans. There are many records from the nineteenth and early twentieth centuries of sites in caves and crevices in cliffs and rock faces, along the coast, on the banks of lakes and rivers and in mountainous areas inland. Now, Swallows in North America use mainly buildings and bridges, as they do in the Old World. The relatively new concrete bridges, rather than the old wooden ones, are particularly liked, and road-expansion programmes have allowed Swallows to colonize new areas. Relatively few natural sites are now known.

Some natural sites may be overlooked by human observers, as they are sometimes in inaccessible and remote areas, but this is not likely to be a serious bias in our knowledge of nesting sites. Clearly, Swallows have taken advantage of the new nesting opportunities we have unwittingly provided and now usually nest on or in our artefacts. They may benefit from this in several ways: sites on buildings may be safer from predators; the substrate may be better and allow nests to stay up for longer, which in turn would save the birds' time and energy otherwise spent building new nests; and nest sites in buildings may be better protected from the weather, and thus more favourable for females incubating eggs and for nestlings. Mud for building the nest is also often available in puddles on tracks and around farm sites. Swallows' food supply, insects, may also be abundant around human habitation, especially where there are livestock and rubbish and manure piles to attract flies.

Farm buildings make good breeding sites.

Living with humans, nevertheless, has its down side, too. Some humans object to the mess deposited under nests by the nestlings and take the nests down. In addition, farmyard marauders such as cats and rats are likely to be present, and some buildings, especially those with metal roofs, can get too hot for the nestlings in summer. Finally, modern farms, with intensively reared animals and widely used pesticides, provide few insects and are not suitable for Swallows.

Overall, however, our own construction work and traditional farming practices have allowed Swallows to colonize areas that would otherwise be entirely unsuitable, with few or no nest sites and a poor supply of insects. Before humans built structures suitable for nesting on, Swallows must have been much less numerous, and restricted to open grassland, mountains, rivers, lakes and coastlines with trees, banks, cliffs or caves for nest sites.

Feeding habitat

The preferred feeding habitats change with the season and with the weather; some may be a good source of insects in midsummer or in sunny weather, while others are best early in the year or when it is cold, wet and windy. When they first arrive on the breeding grounds, Swallows will linger at particularly good feeding areas such as a loch, a pond or a sewage farm for a day or two, depending on the weather and insect activity, before moving on to a place to breed. Once breeding is under way, favoured areas for feeding are open grasslands such as pasture, parkland, or the traditional village green. In contrast, water, trees and hedges, sheltered areas around buildings and manure heaps make good feeding habitat during inclement weather. Once breeding is over and the Swallows are no longer tied to the nest site, they can forage more widely over the countryside. In stormy autumn weather, however, shelterbelts and water are still vital sources of

25

Waterbodies are important feeding sites in bad weather.

insects for Swallows, which need to feed up for the long flight south. In autumn, they also need safe roosting places such as reedbeds and willow scrub, away from predators and disturbance.

Swallows spend their winter as nomads in the southern hemisphere, at altitudes of up to about 3000 m, wandering to wherever they can feast on insects. As on the breeding grounds, water is a favourite feeding area, and reedbeds also provide roosting sites, while large mammals such as zebras and buffalos take the place of horses and cattle as foci of insect activity on the grasslands. Wintering Swallows choose the same sort of country as they did when breeding – open areas where they have room to hunt insects, such as open or bushy grassland, and forest or woodland edge.

Habitat changes and conservation

The Swallow is one of 200 species of European conservation concern identified by BirdLife International, despite being so widespread and common. The reasons for the recent decline in Europe are not clear, but it is probably at least partly due to changes in farming practices, particularly to modern intensive systems, leaving Swallows no other suitable sites for nesting. Climatic variation, especially in the wintering areas, may also be significant. In North America, in contrast, modern farming practices have probably had less effect because of the abundant nest sites provided by highway bridges and culverts.

Swallows rarely come into direct conflict with humans. Occasionally they unwittingly build their nests in a less than convenient place, such as in a garage over a prized vehicle, where their droppings are unwanted. In such circumstances humans may tear down the nests, although nailing up a board beneath them to catch the offending material may be sufficient to cure the problem. In general, however, Swallows are a welcome adjunct to rural life and suffer only inadvertently from our activities. Indeed, some people are very protective towards 'their' pair of Swallows and go out of

The different races vary mainly in the colour of the belly and the extent of the chest-band.

savignii

transitiva

gutturalis

tytleri

erythrogaster

Hilary Burn

their way to provide access to nesting sites for the birds in spring and to protect them and their offspring during summer. People may also welcome them as a means to keep down insects. In the past, too, superstitions that harming the Swallow or its nest brought bad luck (see Chapter 9) have protected it. Even as recently as the 1930s in Britain, A. W. Boyd noted that Swallows in Cheshire and Hereford were protected on that account, and in Anglesey by their effectiveness at removing flies from cowsheds. Farmers these days, however, are less likely to take note of such folklore, and consider flies a sign of poor hygiene; their present farming practices are also detrimental to insect-eating birds.

Farms have been transformed over the past fifty years both because of new technology and because of changes in national and European agricultural policy. Intensive arable farming with its use of pesticides and fertilizers took over from small mixed farms and traditional crop rotation, fields became larger, and many hedgerows have gone. Farmers were given a guaranteed market and there were incentives for them to increase production, with the result that the now notorious surpluses were created. Milk quotas were introduced into the European Community in 1984, with a consequent decline in the numbers of cows kept. A change from livestock to arable production is itself detrimental. In Denmark, Swallow populations were affected when beef and milk production was abandoned: because Swallows prefer to nest on farms where cattle are kept, they lost suitable places to breed.

Improved farm hygiene, intensive livestock-rearing, hedge removal and land drainage are all likely to reduce both the supply of insects that the Swallow needs and the range of feeding sites available. Although it is unclear how much effect they have on Swallows directly, the use of pesticides has also banished their insect food from the fields. Widespread use of the pesticide DDT was implicated in the disappearance of Swallows from the coastal plain of Israel in the 1950s. Modern pesticides may have a less dramatic effect, but, together with other modern agricultural techniques, they could play a role in the Swallow's decline. Nest sites on modern large farms are also scarce, because old brick outbuildings are replaced with modern steel-framed constructions which are unsuitable for the attachment of a mud nest.

In a study in central Westphalia in Germany, Karl-Heinz Loske and Wolf Lederer implicated the destruction of feeding areas on farms and the modernization of farm buildings in a local drop in numbers of Swallows. The population declined by 64.7 per cent between 1978 and 1986, owing to an increase in the number of unhatched eggs and dead chicks, a decline in the proportion of second clutches laid and a consequent reduction in the number of fledglings produced per pair. The decline was not due simply to a change in the weather, although the weather in May and June worsened in the early 1980s; rather, the loss of feeding sites suitable for the Swallows to use in bad weather, such as windbreaks provided by trees and patches of water, made hunting prey in such conditions more difficult. In extreme cases the Swallows were hunting 3.5 km from the nest site, more than three times further than normal.

The percentage of the area used as arable land increased from 7 per cent in 1970 to 62 per cent in 1980, while the number of willow trees, much used as feeding sites by the Swallows, fell from 545 to 271. In addition, farm buildings became less suitable as breeding sites; they were more hygienic and more intensively used, less straw was used as a floor covering, and cow stalls were converted to pig stalls. Traditional manure heaps were replaced by containers of liquid manure, and insecticides were regularly sprayed inside buildings. Swallows will hunt flies around buildings, especially sheltered walls, and over manure heaps in bad weather, so they lost these feeding sites as well. Loske and Lederer also found that modern pig stalls were unsuitable for breeding Swallows, with windows being closed in cold weather and fledglings that landed on or near the ground being trampled by the pigs.

Changes in climate, however, particularly in the wintering areas and perhaps also while the birds are migrating, have also pushed the decline in numbers of Swallows in Europe. A continued drought in South Africa in the past decade, resulting in a dearth of insects for Swallows to eat, has contributed to the decline in Denmark, and probably elsewhere. Anders Møller studied the causes of mortality in a population of Danish Swallows between 1970 and 1988. This population fluctuated in size in the 1970s but then declined in the latter half of Møller's study, the mortality being correlated with rainfall in the wintering areas: more birds died when the weather was dry. During the population decline, the Swallows laid smaller clutches (those birds surviving to breed may have arrived back in poor condition and been unable to lay large clutches). This reduction in breeding performance would in turn exacerbate the population decline.

Climatic factors may play the greater role in regulating populations of breeding Swallows throughout their range, but it is likely that changes in agricultural practices in Europe have made matters worse. An inadequate food supply and lack of suitable nesting and feeding sites on modern farms could prevent populations regaining their numbers after suffering high mortality on the wintering grounds and on migration.

Populations of many farmland species, including Grey Partridges, Linnets, Bullfinches, Corn Buntings and Skylarks, are declining in Britain. For these, as well as for Swallows, traditional, extensive methods of farming need to be maintained and promoted to provide suitable habitat in the future. Swallows need farms where livestock, especially cattle, are reared extensively. A reduction in the use of pesticides and the preservation of hedges, trees, headlands around fields and wetland areas would also improve feeding conditions for them. Recent changes in European agricultural policy, with land being taken out of intensive production, and the setting-up of Environmentally Sensitive Areas, are a promising sign that farmland habitats will be better in future for birds such as the Swallow, but present farming practices are still a long way short of being beneficial for farmland birds.

3

FOOD AND FEEDING BEHAVIOUR

'She flicks past, ahead of her name,
Twinkling away out over the lake.
Reaching this way and that, with her scissors,
Snipping midges'
Ted Hughes

The Swallow eats insects, and almost nothing but insects. It is difficult to see what it is feeding on as it skims over a field, so we know rather little about the diet of adults. It is possible, however, to find out what a Swallow has been eating from its droppings. The wings and hard outer skeleton of insects pass through the bird undigested. Since each group of insects has a distinctive pattern of veins on the wings, they can be identified from these remains, sometimes even to species. So, by patiently sifting through a lot of droppings, I was able to piece together clues to what the Swallows at Stirling were eating.

Flies, especially large ones such as bluebottles and hover-flies, made up 70 per cent of the adults' diet and beetles another 26 per cent; some other insects, especially mayflies, parasitic wasps and aphids, were also taken. David Waugh, also at Stirling but a few years before my own study, identified the prey of Swallows throughout the breeding season from their droppings. He found that 82 per cent of the diet, of adults and nestlings combined, consisted of flies, 12 per cent of beetles, 5 per cent of parasitic wasps, flying ants and similar insects (a group known as Hymenoptera), and 1 per cent of plant bugs and other insects.

On the wintering grounds in Africa, Swallows also eat a variety of insects and other small creatures including grasshoppers, termites, bugs, adult moths and butterflies and caterpillars, flies, parasitic wasps, ants, beetles, spiders and sandhoppers, but David Waugh found that winged ants and other Hymenoptera are much more important than in the summer diet, comprising nearly half of the items taken. Beetles are also important in Africa, forming 30 per cent of the diet, whereas flies make up only 8 per cent. Swallows wintering in Malaysia have a similar diet, as David Waugh and Chris Hails recorded. Here, they also eat mostly flying ants and similar insects (82 per cent of the diet), especially just prior to their return home in late March and early April: as in Africa, 8 per cent of the diet is flies, but only 6 per cent consists of beetles, while a few termites and other insects are also eaten. This difference between summer and winter diets probably reflects a greater availability of ants and similar insects in the wintering areas, making them more economical to catch than large, fast-flying flies. A swarm of ants rising high above the ground provides a profusion of easy-to-capture prey. Hence, they may be a useful food for Swallows that are moulting their wing and tail feathers and so are less manoeuvrable than usual, and especially so when the birds need to build up their fat reserves to start the return journey home.

Swallows rarely eat plants, at least intentionally, but occasionally berries or seeds are an important local food in extreme weather or in winter when insects are scarce. In North America, there are records of flocks of Swallows descending on bushes to take berries such as elder-berries. In the Cape of South Africa, the arillate seeds of acacia trees are commonly eaten, the birds perching or hovering to pluck them; only the fruit-like aril is digested: the seed is discarded in droppings or regurgitated.

More is known about the diet of the nestlings than that of the adults. By putting a loose collar around a chick's neck it is possible to prevent it swallowing the large ball of food given to it by the parent. One can then take a chick from the nest just after it has been fed, and gently remove the ball of food from its throat. The chick is not harmed and need lose only an occasional meal. At Stirling, parent Swallows caught an enormous variety of insects and other small creatures to feed to their nestlings: mayflies, damselflies, stoneflies, grasshoppers, barklice (relatives of booklice), plant bugs such as greenfly, adult moths and butterflies and caterpillars, caddis flies, lacewings, ants, parasitic wasps, bees, beetles, spiders and, most important of all, flies ranging from long-legged craneflies and tiny midges to bulky horse-flies and bluebottles. Spiders may seem a surprising element of the diet, as they have no wings, but they are so light that they can easily travel in a breeze, where a Swallow can pick them up. Studies elsewhere reveal a similar mix of insects in the Swallow's diet, although the exact species differ between areas and between years.

Other types of food are recorded only exceptionally: Swallows have been known to pick up bread from the ground, probably to feed nestlings, and once a stickleback from the water's surface. Parents also give young nestlings grit, particularly calcareous grit, small snail shells and pieces of eggshell, which may help break down the hard outer covering of insects and provide some extra calcium for their growth.

Many of the insects mentioned above, however, are minor items in the diet, caught only rarely and often in special circumstances when more desirable prey are unavailable or more difficult to catch. I have often seen Swallows catching large moths, for example, late in the summer at dusk or in inclement weather when other insects were not flying. A moth fluttering around a light or at a lit window may be an easy catch; these insects however, are difficult for a Swallow to handle, and I have sometimes seen escaped moths crawling around or underneath a Swallow's nest.

Swallows have been accused of plundering hives of bees; in Chaucer's *Parliament of Fowls*, the Swallow is described as a 'murderer of the fowles small/that maken honey of flowers fresh of hue'. However, I found that bees are rarely taken, probably because the bird may be stung. Those bees that are taken are usually the non-stinging males (drones). They may sometimes be a useful food, though, as they are active at lower temperatures than are flies and so may be the only prey available early in the morning or when the weather is cool and other insects are not flying. Few insects are actually avoided, even ants and sepsid flies (small ant-like flies) which are unpalatable to some birds such as Pied Wagtails. I rarely recorded Swallows catching dung-flies, however, even though these were abundant in the cattle-grazed pastures in which the birds usually hunted. Hover-flies, in their striking black and yellow dress, might be thought to be protected by their resemblance to wasps and bees but Swallows are not fooled and at Stirling they took large quantities of these insects. Some insects, such as dragonflies, are probably too fast to be caught easily and too large to be fed to nestlings; the only prey of this type I noted at Stirling were the more delicate damselflies, which fly more weakly than the dragonflies proper, although the latter do occasionally appear on the menu elsewhere.

Swallows sometimes take advantage of a superabundant source of certain prey that they would otherwise hunt only rarely. Some insects, for example, form swarms, providing plenty of prey in a small space for an aerial predator to cash in on. Mayflies emerge as adults from their nymphal stage in large numbers, midges dance in mating swarms, and flying ants leave their nests in streams. In some years, aphids reach plague proportions and rise above the ground en masse. All are hunted by Swallows.

At Stirling, early one summer, the Swallows on one farm collected large numbers of moth larvae for their nestlings, although they rarely caught them at other times. The most common was that of the moth *Ypsolopha parenthesella*, which occurs mainly on oak and birch; when disturbed, it hangs down on a thread from the leaf on which it has been feeding. This behaviour may protect the larvae from predators on the tree, but it makes them easy for a Swallow to snap up. Indeed, the birds may have disturbed the larvae by brushing against the foliage of the tree.

Although any flying insect may be snapped up by a Swallow out hunting, the mainstay of the nestlings' diet is flies, most of them large, stout-bodied insects such as bluebottles, robber-flies, horse-flies and hover-flies. A half-grown brood of five nestlings can put away more than 6000 of them in a day. At Stirling, over the whole breeding season, flies made up 76 per cent of the nestlings' diet, plant bugs and barklice another 19 per cent, moths 3 per cent, and ants, bees and parasitic wasps 1 per cent. Beetles are quite important for adults, but are not brought to the nestlings in large numbers: they made up only 1 per cent of the diet. A few other insects and spiders completed the menu. Other studies have found a similar preponderance of flies. Ivana Kozena, for example, found that Swallows in the Czech Republic had a diet of 62 per cent flies, 28 per cent plant bugs, 4 per cent ants, bees and parasitic wasps, 4 per cent beetles, and a few other insects and spiders. In central Westphalia, Karl-Heinz Loske found that flies made up 66 per cent of the diet, plant bugs 9 per cent, beetles 5 per cent and mayflies 9 per cent.

The nestlings' diet changes during the summer, however, partly because some insects are more abundant at certain times than at others. At

Stirling, for example, early in the summer when first broods were being reared, 81 per cent of insects taken were flies. Very large flies such as bluebottles were taken more commonly at this time, the proportion dropping from five out of ten insects to less than one in ten by the end of August. Large, fast-flying insects are most active at high temperatures, and so may be more difficult to catch in the warm weather of late summer, while at the same time other smaller prey such as swarming greenfly and barklice provide plentiful and easy-to-catch meals. The Swallows increased the proportion of these prey in their diet from one in ten to one in four during the summer, and flies made up only 69 per cent of the diet of second broods. Bees are also more popular prey late in the season, when the stingless drones leave the hives. Seasonal changes in diet are typical in other localities, too. In central Westphalia, for example, muscid flies (such as house-flies), mayflies and dance-flies were important prey in June, whereas plant bugs, hover-flies and snipe-flies were the main prey in July, and more small prey, predominantly march-flies and hover-flies, in August.

As well as changing with the season, the numbers, kinds and sizes of insects taken vary a great deal hour by hour and day by day, from year to year and from area to area. Much depends on the weather, which can determine how abundant a particular type of insect is and whether it can be found conveniently near to the nest. On a cool, wet day in midsummer, for example, large flies become sluggish and remain hidden in vegetation. Swallows are then unable to find them and have to rely on smaller, thin-bodied flies such as fungus gnats, blackflies and midges. At Stirling, tiny flies like these made up three-quarters of the nestlings' diet in bad weather but only a few per cent in warm, sunny weather.

Even at the same site, the diet varies between years. In central Westphalia, for example, Swallows caught flies and aphids more often, and other plant bugs less often, in a cool, wet year than in a dry, warm one; and at Stirling, David Waugh found that 23 per cent of the diet consisted of hover-flies – insects that are typically active in fine weather – in warm dry summers whereas in my study these insects made up only 9 per cent of the diet in cooler, wetter ones. The local habitat is also important in determining the diet. Thus, one of my pairs of Swallows was close enough to a river to collect mayflies, while another pair on an adjacent farm was just a bit too far away for hunting them to be worthwhile.

Although a Swallow clearly has catholic tastes, it does not take just any insect, or just any fly for that matter, that it comes across, and it does not just skim through the air with its bill open to scoop in any insects in its path. Swallows carefully choose their prey. At Stirling, I compared what the Swallows were eating with what was available on the farms where they were breeding. I hunted insects myself, with a butterfly net, sweeping it through the air in the same sort of places in which the Swallows were feeding. The Swallows did not hunt the most abundant insects: I caught mainly very small flies, weighing less than those on the birds' menu. Even when, according to my butterfly net catches, small insects such as midges and aphids were more numerous than large, heavy ones such as horse-flies, hover-flies and bluebottles, the Swallows still picked out the latter.

I found that the more large, heavy prey were available the more the Swallow chose to prey on them mostly ignoring smaller, lightweight insects.

One large insect provides a lot more energy and protein than one small insect, so it pays the Swallow to go after the former. David Waugh showed that the linear dimensions of an insect are not so important to a hunting Swallow as its weight and flying ability. The insects eaten by Swallows at Stirling ranged mostly from 5 – 14 mm in length (though the largest known prey include dragonflies 50 mm long), but insects of a given length can present quite different problems and rewards as target prey. A large, slow cranefly, for example, is much easier to catch than a fast-flying horse-fly of the same length, but may provide a less substantial meal. At the other extreme of the size range, an aphid, which barely flies under its own power, is also very easy to pick out of the air but, although nutritious, by itself it is hardly big enough for a snack.

Usually only when large prey are relatively scarce do Swallows concentrate on small insects. However, they do not completely ignore small prey. I have known Swallows hunting large flies to take some small flies and aphids if they find an abundant source of them. Aphids foolishly swarming in the path of a hunting Swallow are well worth cleaning up. In addition, although Swallows prefer large prey, they do not take the biggest flies around, which may be too fast and difficult to catch. David Waugh also showed that the prey selected for the nestlings are larger on average than those which adult Swallows choose for themselves, probably because the long trip to and from the nest makes it more economical to catch and carry the large insects while eating the small ones en route.

It takes enormous numbers of insects to feed a group of Swallows on a farm. Each brood will have eaten some 150,000 insects by the time it fledges when 20 or 21 days old. The parents may have two broods, exceptionally three, and of course they and the fledglings need insects by the thousands, too. Over the summer, more than a million insects on a farm can go into producing more Swallows. Many of these insects, such as weevils, horse-flies and aphids, are unwelcome on farms, so Swallows are potentially a useful part of a natural pest-control programme. A study in North America also identified a number of species eaten that were pests of crops or timber, such as the cotton boll weevil and rice weevil. The effect of Swallows on insect populations is not known but there is some evidence that large groups reduce the abundance of insects locally (see Chapter 5). Unfortunately modern farming techniques, with lots of pesticides being used, large arable fields and intensively reared livestock, often mean that there are few insects left for hungry Swallows (see Chapter 2).

Hunting insects for the nestlings

Travelling out from the nest to a feeding site, catching an insect, and going all the way back is rather a waste of energy, and time. While the bird is out hunting, it seems more sensible to capture lots of insects. Indeed, Swallows rarely take just a single insect back to the nest. They may do so if they have captured a large moth or other prey that is difficult to hold and would probably be lost if the bird tried to grasp something else as well, but usually the prey are small enough for the Swallow to pack several into its throat to form a ball of food. Sometimes a ball will consist of two or three large flies, or it will contain dozens of small insects or a mixture of large and small prey. In good weather just a few large insects are caught, while in bad weather, when these are scarce, many small insects may need to be collected on each hunting trip to make a meal large enough to be worth taking back to the nestlings. On average, the Swallows at Stirling collected eighteen insects before returning to the nest, but in bad weather they sometimes waited until they had a hundred or more before they delivered them. As with the type of insect hunted, the numbers caught during a hunting trip can vary widely within a season, in different years and in different areas. In Loske's study in central Westphalia, for example, Swallows also collected between one and 102 insects per trip, and again more in cool, cloudy weather, but with an average of only nine insects; and in Kozena's study in the Czech Republic an average of fourteen insects was collected per trip.

As well as the number of insects caught per trip, the weight of the meal carried back to the nestlings also varies. At Stirling, each meal weighed about 0.1 – 0.5 g, averaging 0.27 g. Gareth Jones found that males at Stirling collected smaller meals than females, perhaps because their long

A Swallow catches several insects at a time and keeps them in its throat before returning to its chicks.

35

tails make them less efficient at hunting (see Chapter 5). Small meals are also brought to young nestlings, which do not need so much food as older ones and anyway could not swallow a large mouthful; parents rarely split a ball of food between nestlings, and then only when the nestlings are one or two days old. In Jones's study, once the nestlings were about eight days old, the size of their meals did not change much.

The size of meals varies, however, according to local conditions: in central Westphalia, Loske found that the balls of food were generally smaller than at Stirling, averaging 0.1 g, and containing insects that were mostly no more than 6 mm long, and nestlings were brought smaller meals as they got older. The weather is an additional but variable factor: Swallows in central Westphalia brought smaller balls of food to the nest in sunny than in wet weather, whereas those at Stirling were able to collect some very large meals in good weather. Less food is also collected per trip as the breeding season progresses and more smaller prey are taken.

My Swallows at Stirling usually took less than three minutes to go to a feeding site and collect enough insects for a meal, but they sometimes stayed out for two or three times as long. They also took longer in bad weather, six minutes on average, when they had to find many small insects, than in good weather, when they could catch a throatful of a few large insects in under two minutes. When insects were plentiful they could collect 0.6 kilojoules (0.14 kcalories) worth of food per minute, but in poor conditions they struggled to get about 0.2 kilojoules (0.05 kcalories).

Gareth Jones found that parents feed themselves on over 40 per cent of hunting trips, and spend increasingly more time doing so on trips longer than four minutes. Swallows need about 110 kilojoules of food each day when rearing nestlings, so in bad weather they have to spend much of the day just feeding themselves. They have to put their immediate survival first for as long as the nestlings rely on them; if they starved, so would their brood. Males, however, spend even more time on feeding themselves in bad weather, and less on the brood, than females do: females put themselves more at risk in order to look after the nestlings.

There may be several reasons why the male takes the safer option. Firstly, the male may simply need to spend longer hunting because his long tail makes him less efficient than his partner at catching insects. He is also less likely to be concerned if the brood fails, at least early in the season, since it is easier for him to mate again, perhaps with another female, than for his partner to regain sufficient weight to be able to start another clutch of eggs. In addition, the male may not be sure whether all the chicks in the nest are actually his and whether, therefore, it is worth the effort of feeding them in bad weather (see Chapter 5). Either way, he has less to lose than the female by neglecting the nestlings.

Feeding techniques

Swallows catch most of their prey in mid-air while in flight, homing in on particularly good sources of insects. They will, for example, skim around livestock or follow a tractor to catch the insects that the animal or vehicle has put to flight. Animals, including humans, provide a useful source of food because not only do they flush out insects from the vegetation as they walk, but they also attract bloodsucking insects such as midges or horse-flies. On a hot summer's day I have often been the centre of attention of one or more Swallows jinking around me and snapping up the flies, although the same birds would be just as keen to dive-bomb me as they would a cat if I went close to a nest. On the Swallow's wintering grounds large mammals are used in a similar way, and there are also records of Swallows gathering around flocks of other birds, including Starlings and Ruffs, taking flies and other insects disturbed by them.

Other feeding techniques are not used very often, and then generally as a last resort when the weather is cold or wet and flying insects are not available. They are used particularly early or late in the year, when the Swallows first return to their breeding sites or just before the autumn migration. Swallows are not at home on the ground and could not easily run after prey but there are nevertheless many records from throughout the year of their foraging on the ground, for example on beaches, where they feed on accumulations of sandhoppers and flies. They probably do this mostly when they have come across an aggregation of small prey that can be picked up easily without being chased.

Swallows also sometimes land on plants to pick off insects, such as flies or caterpillars, from the vegetation, or rarely to pick berries. There is even a record of Swallows perching on pigs to feed on insects on the animals' backs, and another of a Swallow perching beside a spider's web and plucking insects from it. Swallows will also hover or swoop low to pick up insects directly from the ground, walls, vegetation or water. Dead or emerging insects on the surfaces of lakes, ponds or even the sea along the coast can be a useful source of food. Artificial lights are also exploited, especially at dusk when moths flutter around them; one pair nesting by a light was able to use it to catch insects by night, long after their usual roosting time. As mentioned above, Swallows when flying near trees sometimes brush against the foliage and then catch the insects, such as

Swallows often feed on insects put to flight by large animals, such as these grazing cows.

In bad weather, a Swallow will often hover to pick up insects from plants.

adult moths and larvae, that they have disturbed; whether this is accidental or the birds learn how to disturb the insects is not known. Fires generate another source of food, especially grass fires in Africa, putting many insects to flight which Swallows can then easily catch. Finally, stealing should be listed among the feeding techniques: there is a record of a Swallow taking a butterfly from a sparrow.

Flight costs and speed

The Swallow is adapted in various ways to hunt and capture large insects. It has a wide, deep bill which is particularly strong and therefore good at grasping large, struggling insects. The wings are long and narrow relative to the weight of the bird, so they provide plenty of lift and reduce drag, making flight very efficient and economical. For birds in general, flying is costly because the muscles use up a lot of energy to flap the wings, but the shape of the Swallow means that these costs are kept low so that the bird can stay in the air most of the day hunting insects. The long, forked tail makes the bird highly manoeuvrable, allowing it to fly slowly, check

The parents bring a throatful of food to the nest every few minutes in good weather.

39

and turn rapidly when pursuing insects. The shape of the tail is important: being triangular when spread, a forked tail, and particularly the long outer feathers, increases the supporting area and provides plenty of lift. It acts like two long airplane flaps: the two halves of the tail maintain a smooth flow of air over the wings, so delaying the point at which the bird would stall, without increasing the drag. A shallowly forked tail is best; if the fork is very deep, the outer feathers are so long that they produce more drag and are therefore a slight disadvantage. Male Swallows have longer tail feathers than females and so are aerodynamically not so perfect, but their tails are affected not only by aerodynamic considerations but also by the females' preference for mating with long-tailed males (see Chapter 5).

The speed of Swallows is legendary: Shakespeare wrote 'True hope is swift, and flyes with Swallowes wings'. Their zigzagging, soaring flight, however, is deceptive and, when feeding, Swallows are by no means among the fastest of birds. David Waugh and I tried timing them using stopwatches and came up with speeds of 5.5 to 18.8 m per second (averaging 10 – 11 m/s). Other researchers in Canada measured the speed of flight of Swallows more accurately using a Doppler radar handgun. They recorded average speeds of 8.6 m/s (range 5 – 18 m/s) for birds flying below 0.5 m, whereas those flying higher than this were timed at 6.8 m/s (range 5 – 11 m/s). The fastest speed recorded is 22 m/s. To catch large, fast-flying insects, Swallows need to be fairly fast but not exceptionally so. David Waugh calculated that the mean speed of the Swallows' favourite prey, horse-flies and hover-flies, is only 5 m/s. Other small birds such as Chaffinches and Starlings can do just as well as Swallows at 9 – 14 m/s and the fastest bird is the Peregrine, which has been recorded by radar to dive for prey at more than 50 m/s (180 km/hr).

When hunting, Swallows fly faster than one would expect if they were trying to travel for as long or as far as they could for a given amount of fuel – they may sacrifice economy for improved efficiency at hunting large prey. They are active flyers, flapping for most of the time, rather than gliding as, for example, House Martins will do. Over the whole breeding season I recorded Swallows that were hunting insects gliding for only about 20 per cent of the time. They often glide when feeding on small, aggregated, weak-flying prey high in the air, and this may account for the slower speeds when the birds fly high. Gliding requires very little energy – the muscles need only hold the wings outstretched – and so this type of flying helps the bird to cut its overall energy costs and is used particularly in bad weather when food is scarce.

How much energy is required for flying depends on the weight of the bird: heavy birds use up more fuel. Both male and female Swallows are heavy at the start of the breeding season, when they have plenty of fat on them, but they lose weight while breeding, especially in bad weather. However, although Swallows do lose weight when hunting is difficult, the seasonal weight loss is not necessarily due to their being unable to find enough food. Parents may deliberately lose weight so that they are more efficient at flying at times when they have lots of hunting to do.

Feeding sites

On warm, sunny days in summer, large flies are active and abundant, visiting plants or manure, searching for mates or hunting prey of their own. Swallows can then hunt best by flying low over open ground. At Stirling, David Waugh found that about 40 per cent of their hunting took place just a metre or so, and a further 20 per cent at 4 – 15 m, above open areas such as pasture; and they concentrate their hunting here on warm days, although they will occasionally hunt higher up, too. The rest of the time they feed over water or around trees and bushes.

Cold, wet and windy weather is inimical to flying insects, which need the warmth of the sun to be active. Large insects then remain out of reach in the vegetation, and others may be restricted to certain sites such as low over water or, when it is windy, they may be found sheltering or windblown in the lee of a hedge, a line of trees or a wall. Swallows usually do about 20 per cent of their hunting low over water, but spend a third of their hunting time there when the weather is poor and large flying insects scarce. The vicinity of trees and other tall vegetation is also useful as a feeding place; in windy weather Swallows spend a quarter of their hunting time in the lee of shelterbelts.

Swallows feeding are an integral part of weather lore. Swallows feeding low are meant to presage rain. Virgil wrote:

'Wet weather seldom hurts the most unwise;
So plain the signs, such prophets are the skies'
The swallow skims the river's watery face;
The frogs renew the croaks of their loquacious race.'

And Thomas Gray wrote:
'When Swallows fleet soar high and sport in air
He told us that the welkin would be clear.'

Both Virgil and Gray were only partly right. Swallows rarely fly high, anyway, and Swallows skimming low, whether over land or water, do not necessarily indicate bad weather. In inclement weather they often feed low over water, but in good weather, although they hunt at a greater range of heights, they still concentrate on feeding low down and will still feed over water. In good weather, the Swallow is the specialist ground-level aerial hunter in Britain. Sand Martins and House Martins feed higher up and Swifts above these. In bad weather, however, all the aerial hunters are forced to feed low, although Swifts sometimes just fly out of the area altogether to circumvent it.

The weather also affects how far from the nest Swallows have to travel to find food. Swallows usually feed close by their nests, flying straight out to a suitable area where insects are likely to be found. At Stirling, in good weather, most hunting for insects to take back to the nestlings took place at up to 250 m from the nest, but in bad weather I would have to look further afield to find the parents. They would usually go to a local stretch of river, where they would be joined by Sand Martins; hedges and groups of trees were also popular. Even then, however, the Swallows usually had to travel only up to about 600 m from the nest. The preferred bad weather feeding sites sometimes change with the time of year as different types of insects become available. A springtime emergence of mayflies may make a river a steady source of food for a while, only to be abandoned when other insects appear elsewhere. In Loske's study in central Westphalia, groups of lime trees and a park were well used in August, running water in April, May and September, and woodland edge, trees, hedges and manure heaps in midsummer.

On arrival in spring, Swallows often stay around waterbodies to feed up after their exhausting migration, before moving to local nest sites. Once at the nest sites, they are constrained to feeding nearby to save time and energy, and this is especially so when they have eggs or nestlings that they have to visit every few minutes to incubate, brood or feed. Consequently, as the season progresses, they hunt more and more close to the nest. At Stirling they fed on average 300 m away while building the nest and laying the eggs, but only 140 m away when feeding the second broods. The increasingly good weather also allows them to find food near their nests. Exactly where they feed depends, of course, on the local habitat and food availability. In Loske's study in central Westphalia, for example, the Swallows fed further away than at Stirling; they had to travel on average 812 m in June, decreasing to 237 m in August.

On their wintering grounds, Swallows are less constrained by time and by having to take food back to a nest, so they can wander more widely to hunt, feeding in large scattered flocks of tens or hundreds of birds. The presence of other aerial feeding birds, however, may limit the sites suitable for feeding in (Chapter 8). In Africa, David Waugh recorded Swallows feeding in similar sites to those in Britain, some 8 m above the ground, spending about three-quarters of their time hunting low over open ground and water. They use a smaller range of feeding sites, however, when in Africa, hunting less around tall vegetation. In the more forested landscape of Malaysia, David Waugh and Chris Hails recorded migrant Swallows feeding most frequently in an open area, but they also often feed over the forest canopy. They feed higher on average, nearly 30 m, than migrants in Africa. Feeding at high levels is particularly common just before migration, when the birds hunt flying ants which rise in columns into the air.

4

VOICE

'Foolish prater, what dost thou
So early at my window do
With thy tuneless serenade.'
Abraham Cowley

The twittering of the Swallow is a familiar and pleasant sound in the countryside in spring. A farmyard is hardly complete without at least one Swallow singing on an overhead wire or while gliding effortlessly above. The full song, given only by the male, is usually described as a melodious twittering mixed with a grating rattling. The French use the word *gazouillement* to describe both the Swallow's song and the babbling of a brook. Abraham Cowley, however, in his poem 'The Swallow' was less than complimentary, and the ancient Greeks regarded the song as witless; the poet Philemon once rebuked a chatterbox by saying that at least a Swallow confined its talk to the summer!

The male often sings out in the open, either perched or in flight, near the nest. Both he and the female, however, use a number of other calls. According to *The Birds of the Western Palearctic* (Cramp 1988), on which the following account is largely based, there are seven main groups of calls, excluding the song: the contact call keeps the members of the pair, and later the family, together; the male's enticement call attracts females; an 'it it it' call serves to cement a pair-bond; a whine is used during copulation; threat calls are used to keep intruders away; alarm calls, of low and high intensity, warn of danger; and a distress call is uttered when a bird is handled, or caught by a predator.

The song

The song itself lasts some three to fifteen seconds. When it is slowed down artificially to separate it into its components, we can see that the rapid twittering consists of phrases which run together. Following a rattling sound, there is sometimes a phrase increasing in pitch (an ascending portamento in musical terms). The song often finishes with a two-syllable whistle, 'su-seer', the second part starting at a higher pitch than the first but then falling in pitch. The rattles in the song are sometimes left out, especially when the male first arrives at the breeding site in the spring and has yet to find a mate. He also includes few rattles when he is singing in flight rather than perched.

Males sing to attract females. They sometimes look for a breeding partner very early in the year, even while on migration or in Africa, and

Singing is an important part of the male's display to attract females.

will sing at these times, especially on the return journey north. In Britain, males sing from their arrival in late April throughout the summer and early autumn, until about the beginning of October. They do not stop singing when they have found a partner, but continue until she has laid her eggs and started incubating. The singing then probably serves to warn other males to keep away from the female. While singing, the male usually perches near the nest, perhaps on a wire or roof outside or occasionally on the ground, or flies around the nest site, leaving the female to get on with building the nest or attending to the eggs.

At dawn during the breeding season, Swallows display communally – their version of the dawn chorus. Several birds fly leisurely, high in the air above the nest sites and singing or uttering another call, a contact call, which sounds like 'wid-wid'. They fly like this for up to an hour before dispersing. The function of the display is unknown, but it probably serves to attract females, as unpaired males looking for mates participate in it.

Contact calls and other vocalizations

Contact calls like those uttered during the communal display are quite varied in sound and function. The main contact call is the 'wid-wid' which is typically low-pitched when the Swallow, male or female, is perching, and high-pitched when the bird is in flight. It is used, as its name suggests, to maintain contact with other Swallows, for instance between members of a pair or members of a family. Contact calls are heard when pairs leave to collect nesting materials or to go hunting. A more rapid version of the call sounds like a gentle twittering. It differs from the song of the male in being long and lacking any rattling sounds, and is used by both sexes. This twittering of the female is sometimes thought of as her song, but it is quite distinct from that of the male. Twittering is a mode of greeting a partner that has been away, but is also used frequently by partners when they are together, around the nest and when flying to and from it. It may help strengthen the bond between them. Parents also twitter to their nestlings, perhaps to encourage them to beg for food, and males will twitter after feeding them, while perching on the nest. The male's twitter sometimes precedes a full song. A third type of contact call, a 'tir-huit', is used to entice other members of the pair or family to follow. Females use it to call to their partners when they go out to collect mud or straw for the nest, and to encourage fledglings to leave the nest.

Males use an enticement call, which sounds like 'wi-wi-wi' as part of their nest-showing display (see Chapter 5); it has been likened to a hoarse wheezing or, when uttered very rapidly, to a gate on a rusty hinge. Parents also use it to lure fledglings back to the nest at roosting time. Unpaired males utter a courtship call, 'it-it-it', to females. Calls also play a role in the pre-copulation and copulation behaviour itself. The male calls 'waeae-waeae' when mating, and American females make a whining noise to signal acceptance when a male solicits a copulation.

Swallows have a number of threat, warning and alarm calls in their repertoire. A simple threat to another Swallow to keep away is a loud stuttering 'witt tititti'. If a predator is spotted in the neighbourhood, however, Swallows use a two-syllable call, 'chiir-chiir'. The same call is used between members of a pair when one appears to be angry or annoyed; a female busy incubating her eggs will utter this call when refusing the unwanted attentions of a male. Greater alarm and anger, caused perhaps by a cat prowling close to the nest or another male Swallow invading a bird's territory, is expressed by a distinctive 'zi-wit', the second syllable being higher-pitched than the first. Swallows are very vocal in response to danger, and a number of other calls of alarm or distress have been recorded: a 'dschiddschid' uttered in flight, a 'flüh-flüh' uttered when chased by a Peregrine, a 'dewihlik', 'zibist', 'zetch', or 'tsättsätsä' when a predator is close by, and a 'weer-weer' uttered when a predator (or bird-ringer!) catches a Swallow. A few calls and sounds are difficult to classify. A female has been recorded making a cackling sound on leaving the nest, and incubating or roosting birds will snap their bills rapidly several times. Bill-snapping is also heard during courtship.

The calls of young Swallows

Young Swallows are quite noisy birds. When they first hatch they just lie quietly in the nest, but by the time they are three days old they can use their voice to beg for food from their parents. At first the call is barely audible, a faint 'si'si'si', but it becomes louder and more insistent as the nestling grows until, by fourteen days, it is a clear 'swiet-swiet-swiet'.

When the nestling gets excited as the parents approach with food, the call speeds up in anticipation, sounding more like a ratchet, 'dsched-dsched'. This call develops into the adult contact call at about the time of fledging.

Fledglings have two calls. They still beg for food, calling out 'wee-wee' to a passing Swallow, and fluttering their wings. The call may help the parents find the fledglings if they are hidden among foliage. Young birds, from the age of about a month, also call 'üit-üit' when a predator approaches. Newly fledged birds cannot sing, but they practise and start singing what is known as a subsong when they are about a month old. The subsong is a series of quiet, short phrases, the beginnings of a twitter but without the richness of the full adult song. By the end of summer, mid-August being the earliest recorded, young males can sing like an adult.

Recognizing the nestlings' calls

In some bird species each nestling or fledgling has a distinctive call, different from those of its neighbours. This ensures that the parents deliver food only to their own youngsters. For a colonial bird, finding and identifying its offspring can be a real problem. Sand Martin parents, for example, leave their fledglings in a crèche while they go off hunting for food; the young often line up in long rows on overhead wires, waiting for

Parents leave their youngsters in a secluded spot, away from other families, while they go hunting.

Fledglings beg noisily when their parents return with food.

their parents to return. The adults clearly need to recognize their own fledglings among the throng, and they do this by voice. Even before the youngsters fully leave the nest, recognizing one's own offspring is important. As soon as they can fly, young Sand Martins can easily reach neighbouring burrows, perhaps landing in the wrong entrance hole after the first hesitant flight, and become mixed up with the wrong family. So the Sand Martin has a distinctive begging call by the time it is sixteen days old, before it is ready to fledge. Before that age parents will accept chicks from another nest, but after it they recognize and evict them.

In North America, a close relative of the Swallow, the Cliff Swallow, faces similar problems because pairs build their nests very close together and leave their fledglings in crèches of sometimes hundreds of youngsters. It, too, can recognize its own offspring by voice, and perhaps also by differences in the colour patterns on the face.

In contrast, Swallow parents are unlikely most of the time to come across a situation where other chicks or fledglings become mixed up with their own. Their nests are generally spaced well apart, so fledglings trying out their new flying skills are not often likely to find themselves in the wrong nest. Furthermore, the family keeps itself to itself. Once the fledglings have all left the nest, the parents deposit them in a safe place such as a branch of a tree, by themselves, well away from other family groups, when they go out to hunt. As the fledglings become more mobile in their first two weeks out of the nest, the family groups at a site where several pairs have bred may start to meet and may mix, but even when this happens the fledglings recognize and beg from their own parents when they approach. Consequently, Swallow parents do not need to, and apparently do not, recognize their own offspring. So long as they know where they left them, in a particular nest if they have nestlings or at a place outside if they have fledglings, they will usually find and feed the right ones. This strategy only rarely goes wrong; and it may be a better one for Swallows than trying to identify their own chicks and mistakenly rejecting one of their own. For Cliff Swallows and Sand Martins there is more danger of accepting an alien chick, so identification is necessary.

Parent Swallows will readily accept and care for chicks from another nest. Mandy Medvin and Michael Beecher at the University of Washington, Seattle, tried giving parents (of the North American race) another pair's chicks that were ready to fledge; they found that the parents accepted the alien chicks and looked after them when they fledged. In one case, the parents even tried to retrieve a foster chick which flew out of the nest when it was transferred! In contrast, when Sand Martin chicks are fostered out into another nest, they either leave or are chased out. There are also several records of natural adoptions where newly fledged Swallows have strayed into another nest and been fed by the owners of that nest, particularly where nests are grouped close together. In one case, a pair ended up feeding five chicks of their own plus four fledglings from two other nests. In another, Swallows even fed a fledgling Tree Swallow, a bird with a brown back and white throat, quite unlike a young Swallow, that had temporarily found its way into the nest, showing just how undiscriminating they are.

As well as accepting chicks that are not their own, Swallow parents also seem to be unable to identify their own chicks, of fledging age, in experiments when pre-recorded calls of their own and other chicks are played to them. They do not preferentially respond to the calls of their own offspring. On the other hand, chicks of this age can recognize the calls of their parents, although not so well as young Cliff Swallows or Sand Martins recognize theirs.

The reason why Sand Martin and Cliff Swallow parents can easily recognize the voice of their own offspring while Swallow parents apparently do not lies in the structure of the calls of the young birds. Michael Beecher and his colleagues, having established that adult Bank Swallows (North American Sand Martins) and Cliff Swallows do recognize individual nestlings by voice and that Swallows do not, have recently looked closely at the begging calls of the latter two species. They found that Swallow chicks (again of the North American race) have a less elaborate begging call than Cliff Swallow chicks. Both calls have two, non-harmonically-related frequency bands or 'voices', but in the Swallow's call, the difference between the two frequencies varies less. The Swallow's call also begins less clearly, with a burst of harsh sound, and the frequency modulation is not repetitive as it is in the Cliff Swallow's call. Consequently, the calls of different Cliff Swallows are more easily told apart than are calls of Swallows. In addition, these researchers found that sibling Cliff Swallows have very similar calls, making it easy for their parents to recognize their family. The calls of sibling Swallows, in contrast, are not particularly similar; Swallow parents can tell at a distance that a nestling is a Swallow, but not necessarily whether it is one of theirs.

One of the biologists' experiments investigated how easily adult Cliff Swallows, Swallows and a quite unrelated species, the Starling, could tell apart the begging calls of nestlings of the two swallow species. The scientists trained all three species to discriminate between two tape-recorded calls by rewarding them with food when they indicated by pecking at a particular spot in the experimental apparatus that the calls they heard were different. All three species indicated by their pecking that they could tell whether two Cliff Swallow calls or two Swallow calls were from different individuals, but they could discriminate much faster between two Cliff Swallows than between two Swallows, and Cliff Swallows discriminated between calls faster than did Swallows. So, Swallows do not lack the ability to identify a particular call, and the calls of nestling Swallows are distinct enough for identification to be possible. The apparent inability of parent Swallows in the wild to recognize their own youngsters thus seems to be at least partly a matter of ignoring differences between the calls of nestlings because they do not need to recognize them.

The small group sizes in which Swallows nest, and the segregation of their fledglings from their neighbours, have probably meant not only that they do not need to recognize their offspring but also that vocal communication in the family has become important. Indeed, Swallows have quite a large repertoire of calls. It is not easy to communicate with a partner or offspring at a distance by calling if lots of close neighbours are making a noise at the same time; the call would be lost in the general din. This is why the highly colonial Cliff Swallow, for example, uses only half the number of calls that the Swallow does, and relies more on visual signals; calls are most useful for Cliff Swallows at close range, as when a parent needs to identify the youngster it is about to feed. Charles Brown of Yale University has suggested that vocal confusion is one reason why hybrids between Swallows and Cave or Cliff Swallows have become more frequent in Texas recently. All three species nowadays often nest together in highway culverts – a relatively recent innovation – where there is space for large groups to form. Their twitter songs are similar, are likely to be distorted in culverts, and may be confused in the large, noisy mixed-species groups breeding together, with the consequence that the different species mistakenly pair up with each other.

5

MATING AND
SOCIAL BEHAVIOUR

'All the summer long is the swallow a most instructive pattern of unwearied industry and affection.'
Gilbert White

Over the past ten years or so, our knowledge of the behaviour of birds, including Swallows, has increased enormously. Swallows have been particular favourites for scientific study because their nests are easy of access and they are used to the presence of humans. As a result of such studies, the early reputations of such birds being faithful to each other, industrious and fair-minded have been somewhat tarnished by the knowledge that cuckoldry is rife, males commit infanticide, and females dump their eggs in others' nests, leaving the victim to rear the chick. In the race to pass on their genes to the next generation, birds behave in ways that seem to us selfish, deceitful and manipulative. Of course, their behaviour is driven by mindless evolution and does not imply any reasoning by the birds themselves. Individuals are programmed by their genes to acquire as many mates as possible or mates of the highest available quality (or both) and to maximize the number and quality of the offspring they produce, by whatever means available: failure to do so would be genetic suicide.

Group sizes and territories

Swallows will breed in groups of varying size, but many nest as solitary pairs. Average numbers of pairs recorded breeding together in various studies were 1.14 in England, 3.1 in Denmark, 2.3 in Finland and 5.8 in Germany. At Stirling, there were four pairs on a farm on average, usually in separate buildings or separate rooms within a building. When groups do form, there are usually fewer than five nests at a site, but sometimes there are more. In a large population in Austria, for example, 127 pairs nested by themselves, there were 69 groups of two, 21 groups of three and 22 groups of four to nine. In a Danish study, there were 40 solitary pairs, 27 groups of two, six groups of three, and sixteen groups of four to 22 pairs.

A few very large groups are known: 95 nests were recorded in one stable in Ulm in Germany, over 100 in a railway workshop and there are several records of more than fifty nests in one building. In North America, bridges, large barns and open cow sheds provide room for many nests, often twenty or more. Where there are several suitable buildings at one

A male Swallow scolds and chases a female off his perch.

site, sometimes very large numbers accumulate: there are records of 120 pairs at one farm and 280 at another. In Denmark, Anders Møller found the number of pairs breeding on a farm was related to the area of stables and stalls on it, larger areas having more room for nests. At natural sites, Swallows also nest in solitary pairs or small groups of mostly up to 30 pairs.

Some species of swallow and martin are highly colonial. House Martins and Cliff Swallows, for example, regularly nest in groups of tens or hundreds, even thousands of pairs, and they build their nests adjacent to each other. Swallows, in contrast, as well as usually nesting in ones or twos, also keep their nests apart, often by 3 or 4 m, preferably even in separate buildings. When they do nest close together, they often avoid direct contact with neighbours by placing their nests on opposite sides of a beam and approach them from different directions. They defend a small area, some $4 - 25$ m^2, around the nest, attacking and chasing off other Swallows that come too close. Because they have open nests, they are very much aware of the activities of neighbouring birds and potential intruders. Cliff Swallows and House Martins, on the other hand, have enclosed nests, so they are not disturbed so easily by other birds and can put up with having close neighbours. Living in a group like this has many consequences for individual birds, some good, some bad, and these are discussed further at the end of this chapter.

In many species of birds, pairs live in a territory containing a nest site and ample food resources for rearing the offspring, and which the birds defend from others of the same species. This would not be a sensible arrangement for Swallows, however, because of the nature of their food. Flying insects can be found here and there on a farm, perhaps

51

congregating around some grazing cattle or, on a windy day, aggregating in the lee of a hedge, but the best places for them vary from day to day and sometimes from hour to hour. In addition, at times they can occur in huge numbers, while at other times Swallows may have to hunt over a wide area to find enough. Such a distribution of food makes it difficult and certainly costly in terms of time and energy to defend from other Swallows. Consequently, Swallows concentrate their defence on their nest site, and males also defend their partners; in contrast, they will often share their feeding area with other Swallows.

Swallows are quite aggressive, especially at the nest, both among themselves and with competitors for nest sites (see Chapter 6). When perched they usually keep at least 10 – 15 cm from each other and from other species, although in severe weather they are less aggressive and will huddle together (see Chapter 8). Swallows chasing each other around the yard, skimming close to the ground and in and out of barns, often calling noisily, are a common sight in spring on a farm. The twists and turns of one bird are skilfully matched by the weaving flight of its pursuer. The birds are not playing or courting, however; they have a serious purpose, to keep other Swallows at bay. Both male and female attack Swallows approaching too close to the nest, but males are particularly aggressive towards rival males, which may have designs on their females. When two males threaten each other, they engage in a singing contest, while perched side on to each other with their carpal joints visible and feathers sleeked, heads raised at 45° and pointing in the same direction. Threats and chases may lead to a fight, the males entangling their feet and falling to the ground. These fights can continue until one or other combatant is killed. In one case, a male was forced into a corner in a stable and prevented from leaving for 24 hours, and in another two males fought on and off for over a week. Females also fight with each other, again sometimes leading to the death of one of them.

Acquiring a partner

Swallows are outwardly monogamous, although promiscuity is not uncommon. Two parents are needed to rear a brood of Swallows, so the usual arrangement is for a male to pair up with one female for the duration of the breeding season. They generally stay together for the second clutch of the year, and often for life. Swallows do not usually live for long, however, and it often happens that a partner dies after only one breeding season. In one study in Germany, for example, only thirteen out of 115 pairs lasted two years. For the few long-lived individuals, however, pair-bonds can last a long time: one male is known to have paired monogamously over eleven years, with two partners for four years each and three other partners for one year each.

Not all pairings work out or last very long, though, and some birds get divorced. Sometimes both members of a pair return to the same breeding area in the spring but decide to pair up with different mates, rather than with each other again, and sometimes a newly formed pair will split up

Males perch side-by-side in a threat display,
which may lead to a fight.

even before egg-laying has got under way. Other pairs may decide to go
their separate ways after the first brood has fledged.

Occasionally, and in exceptional circumstances, a male will pair with
two females at the same time, particularly if their nests are close together.
It may happen, for example, that a male dies and a neighbouring male
takes over his partner and nest; or that a male starts out with one partner
but, by aggressively chasing off a paired male from a neighbouring nest, he
acquires a second one; or an unpaired female may visit his nest and
eventually pair with him. If a male has two partners he usually helps to
feed both broods, but mainly his first female's offspring; if he ignores one of
them, the nestlings will probably die despite the efforts of the female.

Obtaining a mate, and not just any mate but the best available, is the
most important task facing Swallows when they arrive on the breeding
grounds. A few return already paired, perhaps meeting their partners on
migration or even on the wintering grounds. As already mentioned, males
sing when still in Africa and are known to display while on migration, so
they are clearly ready to pair early in the year. Most, however, start
looking once they have finished their spring migration. All the females at a
breeding site will be looking for, and will usually get, a partner, but this is
not so for the males. In Anders Møller's study in Denmark, 13 per cent of
males remained without a partner, and in another study as many as one in
five males failed to pair up when they were one year old. Females, rather
than males, size up the available Swallows and choose the best partners

53

A male shows his chosen nest to a female to persuade her to be his partner.

they can get; the less desirable males may therefore find themselves rejected and without an opportunity to breed.

The usual way to find a partner is for a male to select a potential nest site and then to display near it to attract females. Singing is an important part of the display he uses to convince a female to pair with him. He usually arrives at the breeding site before the females do. If he had a partner the previous year, and assuming she is still alive, he may need do no more than start building a nest or repairing an old one before she arrives, or he may just wait for her before he starts building. A male without a partner, however, must show off himself and his chosen nest site to females which are also looking for a partner. Females are very choosy and select a male according to his looks. To show off his best features, a male makes himself conspicuous by flying in circles above the nest site and singing. If he sees a group of Swallows approaching he increases his efforts, singing more loudly, and swooping or spiralling down to the nest site. If a female shows interest in him he lands, continuing to sing, but then adds another call from his repertoire: the enticement call. Females find it attractive and are induced to land near the male, at which point he reverts to his twittering song, which at this time contains prominent rattling sounds. The female's attention now held, he finishes his song with his head turned away from her and then quickly turns it back towards her. Now he directs her attention to the nest or the site chosen for the nest. He lowers his head, again turning away from the female, and pecks at the site. He may repeat this performance at several sites until she is satisfied with one. Even after all this effort on the male's part, however, the female may eventually reject him as not meeting her high standards and may look for a better one. When she has finally chosen a partner and a nest site, she will confirm her willingness to enter into a long-term relationship by roosting at the site. Rarely, the female may choose a site without the male taking the initiative.

The male solicits a copulation from the female by singing to her, usually when she is perching near the nest. The copulation itself can be brief, with few preliminaries. The male flies over to the female, hovers, lands on her back and copulates, calling 'waeae-waeae'. Afterwards she often preens. The whole process is over in seconds. The male also sometimes flutters slowly and spreads his tail wide, showing off the white patches and long streamers, but this is not a necessary prelude to mating. He does not always have his own way, however: a female may reject his advances, by turning or flying away, by threatening him with open bill and raised wings, or by pecking at him. Copulations are not often seen by human observers, but they are known to occur over an extended period from 50 days before egg-laying to the fifth day of incubation, usually in the morning, and particularly from fifteen days before laying starts for the first clutch and eight or nine days before the second clutch.

As I explain later, the male's plumage and voice are important considerations for a female searching for a mate, and he shows these off to her as best he can. If flaunting one's finery and serenading fail to impress the females, however, there are other, 'sneakier', and to human observers sometimes more gruesome, ways of acquiring a partner. Males monitor activities at other nests so that they can choose the best time to act. First, and most innocuously, a male may simply associate with a paired female so that, if her partner dies or her nesting attempt fails, he will be the most likely candidate to be her new partner. He will also know if and when a pair is going to divorce and when females become available as partners if he visits them frequently. Attending nests may also help a young male acquire a nest site in subsequent seasons by helping him to become familiar with the site and with the individuals already nesting there.

Paired males, too, attend other nests, and probably for similar reasons particularly if their own nests have failed. If they know which females are likely to be available as partners and become familiar to them, they can more easily get new partners if their current ones die or desert them. Females less frequently visit nests but they sometimes do so, especially after losing their own clutch or brood. Again, they are probably looking for opportunities to pair up.

A second option for a male, however, is to kill to get a partner. During visits to nests he checks their contents. If he finds one containing nestlings just a few days old he may kill the whole brood. He would peck the nestlings, pick them up, fly a few feet away and drop them on the ground.

Swallows mate quickly with few preliminaries.

With her brood gone, the female may divorce her partner (who has failed to meet her expectations of guardian of the nest) and may then mate with the male who killed her nestlings. A widow with young nestlings is also at risk, since an unpaired male wanting her as a partner may also kill her brood. A male does not want to look after nestlings that are not his own. From his point of view, it is more sensible for him to get rid of them, so the female will be ready to mate with him quickly and bear his own offspring. If he waited until her current brood fledged, it might be too late for him to rear even one brood successfully with her. Infanticide committed to acquire a mate is common among animals. Although in our modern Western society we find it abhorrent, it is just another way of ensuring that a male or female passes on his or her own genes to as many offspring as possible.

It is not just unpaired males that practise infanticide. Males who lose their partners from death or desertion will also try to acquire another by these means. Nevertheless, Swallows are not committed killers which always use these tactics to get what they want. They use infanticide as an occasional means to acquire a partner if the circumstances warrant and allow it. Males who pair normally in some years will commit infanticide in others. In one instance, for example, observed by Janice Crook and William Shields in the Adirondacks in New York State, a male reared broods normally in two years, but in his third year his partner disappeared before the eggs hatched. The male deserted the clutch – he could not have incubated them successfully by himself – and moved to another nest, where he killed four one-day-old nestlings. The victimized female divorced her partner and re-mated with the killer in another nest.

During one study, Anders Møller recorded infanticide in fourteen out of 298 first broods; second broods were not affected, since that late in the breeding season a killer would not have enough time to sire and rear another brood anyway. Møller witnessed infanticide three times and suspected that it had happened at another eleven nests. In eleven cases, it occurred after the male owner of the nest had disappeared and in three when the female was still paired. In twelve cases the killer re-nested successfully later that season with the female whose brood he had destroyed. In their study on North American Swallows, Janice Crooks and William Shields recorded infanticide at eight out of 89 nests, although only four of the males mated with the females they victimized. Clearly, the male's tactics do not always work: if the victimized female just leaves the group and partners another bird, the infanticidal male is left with no reward for the deed. However, it is still a useful strategy for unpaired males to try. In Anders Møller's study, a quarter of unpaired males were able to acquire a partner in this way.

Clearly it is not in the interest of a paired female to have a male kill her offspring but she probably has no say in the matter. It is difficult to guard the nest from such intruders all the time. Guarding the nest is especially difficult if the female has lost her partner and has to collect all the food for the nestlings herself. If she is a widow, finding another partner and having a new clutch may, however, be the best course of action for her anyway, as it would be difficult for her to rear a brood by herself. Mating with the killer of her offspring may seem strange, but it is preferable to not having a partner at all and thus not rearing any fledglings that season.

Guarding the nest certainly helps to reduce the risk of infanticide. Møller found that nests where infanticide occurred were guarded less intensively than other nests (45 per cent of the time, versus 81 per cent). He showed this experimentally by detaining males in captivity for a few hours so that their nests were less well guarded. Unpaired males visited these nests and removed some of the nestlings, whereas no infanticide was seen at nests where males were still guarding. Only nests in groups were affected, however; solitary nests are relatively safe from unwelcome visitors.

A female does have one strategy she could use to prevent infanticide. If she can convince the male intruder that he has fathered some of the nestlings in the nest, he is unlikely to kill them and instead may help to look after them, especially if the female is a widow. She could do this by mating promiscuously with her male neighbours when she is laying the eggs. These males may then care for her nestlings later on. At least one instance of such adoption is known. Swallows are certainly promiscuous, but we do not know how important this is for preventing infanticide. Females who already have a partner usually reject attempts by undesirable, unpaired males to copulate with them, so they clearly do not use promiscuous behaviour with this category of males to prevent infanticide. Mating with the neighbours, however, may be more advantageous.

Not all visitors to nests have such nefarious plans. There have been several anecdotal accounts of individual Swallows helping other pairs to look after nestlings. Early reports assumed that these were juveniles helping to rear their younger brothers and sisters. Later studies showed, however, that the so-called helpers were adults and not related to the pairs they were helping. Mostly these birds just hover at the nest, perch on or near it, or follow the female. They may be monitoring nests or looking for an opportunity to break up a partnership, but they occasionally do helpful things such as mob predators, chase off other intruders, help with nest-building, feed the nestlings and tidy up their droppings. Janice Crook and William Shields recorded one instance where a male even adopted the nestlings at a nest where the original male had disappeared, brooding and feeding them and mobbing predators. Mandy Medvin, Michael Beecher and Sandy Andelman suggested that accounts of adult helpers feeding nestlings may involve first-year birds who have kept a juvenile-like plumage; these young birds may fail to acquire a partner and instead attend the nests of breeding pairs to gain experience of the area and the group. In this way they may be more successful at rearing offspring the following year. Both males and females may also attend nests because of misplaced parental care after their own nests have failed.

Why males have long tails

Although males actively seek an opportunity to mate with a female, it is usually she who decides whether or not to copulate and pair with a particular male. All a male can do is show off to impress her. Females are usually the choosier sex among birds. A female Swallow produces only a few chicks at a time, probably only six to eight in a season, and she naturally wants the best father for them. She needs a partner who is healthy and who will be able to help her feed them, but she also wants one who will pass on 'good genes' so that the offspring will inherit his good qualities, such as his attractiveness to the opposite sex and his ability to withstand disease and parasites. With only a few offspring to perpetuate her genes, it is vital for her to find the right mate. A male, on the other hand, produces large numbers of sperm and can sire many more offspring than a single female can produce, so, although he wants a good partner, he is more interested in the quantity than the quality of the females with whom he copulates.

A female Swallow may be wooed by several suitors at a popular breeding site, and she will visit a number of males before deciding to pair with one of them. Choosing the best of them may seem difficult, but the main guide to a highly desirable male is his tail, with its long streamers, which he fans and shows off when he courts females. Males vary quite a bit in the length of their outer tail feathers, much more so than in general body size. From their first to their second year of life, they grow, on average, a slightly longer tail; but from then on the tail stays roughly the same length. Some males, however, change their tail length considerably. In Anders Møller's study, some males grew tails as much as 19 mm shorter

Males with long tails are highly desirable mates.

than in the previous year, while others grew tails as much as 21 mm longer. Growing a long tail is not easy because it uses up a lot of energy, so males have to be in good condition to do it. Thus, males debilitated by heavy infestations of parasites during the breeding season (see Chapter 6) are unable to increase the length of their tails by much, if at all, during moult in the following winter. The climate on the wintering grounds when the Swallows are moulting is also very important because this determines how much food is available. Good weather in this context means quite wet weather because insects are less abundant during droughts when the vegetation fails to grow. Male Swallows can grow longer tails when there has been plenty of rain and hence there is a bumper crop of insects to eat. A good food supply is particularly important for those males who might be carrying parasites or disease.

Females do not have these problems. Although they do grow a slightly longer tail between their first and second years, the increase is only small and requires relatively little energy. Their tail is already the best size for its purpose – to provide manoeuvrability when hunting large insects in flight for their nestlings – and they do not want to grow a very long tail. Hence, the length of the tail is not affected by whether the female is suffering, say, from a parasite infection or by the weather on the wintering grounds. Males, on the other hand, want to grow their tails as long as they can, at least to an upper limit where they are almost so long that they become an impediment to hunting insects.

It is the longer-tailed males that appear to be the most successful at breeding. It is they who arrive at the breeding site early and quickly attract females. Within a few days they have usually paired up and started nest-building. They get the best partners: the heaviest females in good condition who arrive back in spring early. The long-tailed males benefit from having such good partners, because they can start breeding early, they have time for two broods and so they produce more nestlings. In addition to all these advantages, long-tailed males are also more successful at cuckolding other Swallows (see below).

Females also visit short-tailed males but they often do not stay, so that these males may fail to get a partner. If they are lucky they may find one after several days, perhaps when the longer-tailed males are no longer available for prospecting females, and so they start breeding late and may have time to rear only one brood that season. Other short-tailed males fail to find a partner at all, and they are also rejected by females when they try cuckolding other Swallows. Even for these males, however, having a longer tail than the rivals is an advantage, since the longer-tailed ones among them are still likely to be more successful at getting a partner by committing infanticide.

In an elegant experiment, Anders Møller has shown that females clearly prefer males with long tails. He caught male Swallows and changed the lengths of the streamers by about 20 per cent. He shortened the outer tail feathers of some of the males to 8 cm, by cutting off a piece from the end, and elongated those of others to 12 cm, by attaching an extra piece of feather. Others just had their tails cut and glued back on so they kept more normal tails of 10 cm. Males with artificially long tails were preferred by females, both when they were seeking a partner and later in the season when they were seeking matings promiscuously. They took only about three days to get a partner, while males with shortened tails took four times as long. Males with tails of normal length found a mate in about eight days. Because of their early start, males with elongated tails were more likely to have two broods that season and they produced about eight fledglings, more than twice as many as the males with shortened tails.

Since females prefer males with very long tails, we might ask why we do not see male Swallows with tails 20 or 30 cm long instead of only 10 cm or so. We might expect males with longer tails to be even more desirable, even more successful with the females. Unfortunately, long tails do have a disadvantage. As I mentioned in Chapter 3, very long outer tail feathers produce excessive drag and make flying less efficient. Anders Møller found that males with artificially elongated tails were less adept at flying. They were poorer hunters and could catch only smaller insects than their partners. Probably as a result of a poor diet, their feathers at the next moult were of poor quality, with more frequent fault bars, and the males could grow only short outer tail feathers. As already stated, growing long feathers requires a lot of energy and nutrients (particularly certain proteins that contain sulphur, which are essential components of feathers), and males in poor condition because of an inadequate diet just cannot afford to grow a long tail. Consequently, the males with artificially elongated tails in Møller's study were unattractive to females the following year, took longer to acquire a partner and produced fewer fledglings than males whose tails had been shortened or left untouched. In addition, and again perhaps because of their poor manoeuvrability, males with artificially elongated tails (this time in a study in Ontario in Canada, by Henrik Smith and Robert Montgomerie) seem to be poor at preventing their partners being promiscuous and are cuckolded more frequently than males with shortened tails. They may have to spend more time feeding themselves instead of watching out for philanderers, or they may just be less effective at keeping philanderers at bay. The male Swallow must therefore balance the benefits of pairing early with the costs of harming his ability both to feed himself and to keep other males away from his partner; a reasonably long tail turns out to be preferable to a very long one.

Choosing males with long tails may seem to be a strange way of assessing how desirable a potential mate is. Some biologists have suggested that females choose to mate with males that have extravagant plumage ornaments such as long tails, simply because their sons, in turn, will have long tails and be attractive to females. Alternatively, long-tailed males may, for some reason, make better husbands and fathers. A third possibility is that females are shopping for inherited characteristics – good genes – other than tail length that the male will pass on to their offspring. A long tail would then advertise the fact that a male has these other good genes and is not itself an advantage. On the contrary, it is something of a liability, or handicap, as it makes hunting more difficult, but it may indicate to a female how good a male is. It may reliably show, for example, that a male is healthy, free from parasites and in good condition, because a male in poor health and condition and infested with parasites could not manage to grow such a handicap. Females therefore prefer males with handicaps such as long tails because it assures them that these males have desirable characteristics. Such males are likely to pass on their good qualities to their offspring, making them suitable fathers for a female's next brood.

Long-tailed male Swallows are not, it seems, better husbands and fathers than short-tailed males. They actually feed their nestlings less frequently than short-tailed males, so their partners have to work harder to compensate. Their apparent laziness may simply be a reflection of the long tail making them less efficient at hunting. They catch smaller insects and have to collect more of them to make up a meal to take back to the nestlings. In an experiment on Spanish Swallows, Florentino de Lope and Anders Møller artificially lengthened or shortened the tails of paired males. They found that females paired to males with elongated tails fed the nestlings more frequently than if their partners had shortened tails, to make up for the males' reduced contribution: their partners had to find seventeen small prey per hunting trip on average, while males with normal tails caught thirteen larger prey per trip and males with shortened tails were such good hunters that they could catch large prey, collecting only eight at a time.

So, females clearly do not mate with long-tailed males because they are better parents. Long-tailed males, however, suffer less from parasites and they may be more resistant to them. Naturally long-tailed males are in better condition than short-tailed males, as the fact that they survive better to the next breeding season shows, and growing a long tail during the winter is relatively easy for them. A short-tailed male cannot try to grow a much longer tail without compromising his health and survival to the next breeding season. Consequently, a female is unlikely to be fooled. By choosing a long-tailed male, she is sure to get a good, healthy male relatively resistant to parasites, not an inferior one who has tried to cheat the system.

The length of the tail is an inherited characteristic. Long-tailed males will have long-tailed sons who will, in turn, be healthy and attractive to females, while short-tailed males will have unattractive, parasite-ridden, short-tailed sons. Of course, there is a lot of variability dependent on, for example, how abundant insects are, and a long-tailed male may still do poorly if food happens to be scarce for climatic reasons. In general, however, the fathers' genes for tail length are expressed in their offspring. A female choosing a long-tailed male for a partner, or for an extra mate if she is promiscuous, will thereby ensure that her sons are attractive, healthy and successful males when they are old enough to breed.

Females do not use only the length of the tail as a guide to a male's qualities as a father. The best males also have symmetrical tails: that is the two outer tail feathers are of the same length. It is difficult to grow a symmetrical tail. If food is hard to get or a bird is in poor condition, a male will not have sufficient resources for growing feathers and one streamer may end up longer than the other. Males whose nests are infested with parasites, for example, are unable to grow as symmetrical a tail as that grown by those untroubled by parasites. Short-tailed males find it difficult anyway to grow a long tail, and they are more likely to have an asymmetrical one. Females prefer tails that are symmetrical, as Anders Møller showed in another experiment. To see what sort of tail females preferred, he shortened the tails of some males and lengthened those of others, and also made some more asymmetrical or symmetrical. Long-tailed males acquired partners sooner if they had symmetrical tails than if they had asymmetrical ones. Short-tailed males were also more successful if they had symmetrical tails but they still did less well than long-tailed males. Because they pair up early, males with symmetrical tails rear more offspring than those with asymmetrical ones.

Evidence for the importance of symmetrical tails for males comes from the population of Swallows breeding near Chernobyl, an area contaminated by radioactivity in the spring of 1986. Some males from Chernobyl have since grown aberrant and highly asymmetrical tail feathers (14 per cent have brushy streamers) and they have bred later than males with more normal tails, suggesting that females find them less attractive.

Symmetrical tails are not just ornaments attractive to females. They are necessary for a Swallow to fly and hunt insects efficiently. The shape of the tail is important aerodynamically (see Chapter 3). Most of the lift is provided by the outermost tail feathers; if one is shorter than the other, the lift is reduced and is also greater on the longer side, causing rolling and yawing forces. A Swallow can counter the destabilizing effect of an asymmetrical tail to some extent by changing the position of the tail in flight but he cannot compensate for the loss in lift. Consequently, males

Swallows in North America have shorter tails than those in Europe.

with asymmetrical tails are likely to be less manoeuvrable than those with symmetrical ones. Anders Møller demonstrated this in another experiment. He cut the tails of some males to make them more (or less) asymmetrical; he then dyed the front edge of their wings with a slow-drying ink and released them in a room containing barriers made of netting. The Swallows left a clear, inky mark on the barriers when they brushed past them. Males with asymmetrical tails found it more difficult to avoid the barriers.

Females may, of course, avoid a male with an asymmetrical tail because he cannot fly very well. To test this idea, Møller changed the appearance of the tails of some males by painting a portion of the tail with typing-correction fluid (Tipp-Ex). This made them look as if they had asymmetrical tails when, in fact, they did not, but their manoeuvrability was not affected as it would have been if the tails really were asymmetrical. The females seemed to be misled. Those males with apparently asymmetrical tails took longer to find a partner, and consequently fewer had second clutches and produced fewer nestlings. This experiment shows that the females base their choice of male on his appearance and not on the fact that an asymmetrical tail makes him less manoeuvrable.

Males with asymmetrical tails are clearly at a disadvantage when feeding both themselves and their offspring, but for females their flying ability is not important directly. They are more concerned with what the length and symmetry of the tail tell them about the health and vigour of the male: whether he is going to pass on good genes to their offspring. They certainly do not choose males with symmetrical tails because they are better fathers; Møller has shown that females paired with males who have long, symmetrical tails have to work relatively harder to feed the nestlings than do partners of males with short, asymmetrical tails.

Henrik Smith and Robert Montgomerie showed that North American females also seem to prefer long-tailed males: those males with artificially elongated tails acquired partners and could start laying earlier than males with artificially shortened tails. They found, however, that males with elongated tails did not rear more fledglings than those with shortened tails and were even less likely to have second broods. The outer tail feathers of North American males are naturally shorter than in the European race (only 91 mm, compared with 105 mm in Anders Møller's study). Smith and Montgomerie suggested that this difference is a consequence of the fact that the former help to incubate the clutch, whereas the latter do not (see Chapter 6). North American males, therefore, have less opportunity to philander, and so there is less competition among them to impress and copulate with lots of females throughout the breeding season. Consequently, there is less pressure on them to grow an extravagantly long tail to show off to females. It is more important for them to pair with the best partner they can find at the start of the season, and they can do this even without as long a tail as a European male.

Also, in these North American males, the tail is prone to being damaged, probably during incubation when it may be accidentally brushed against the nest or a wall, and naturally long-tailed males are the most likely to break theirs. The damaged tail may affect a male's chances of being accepted as a partner for a second clutch. In addition, a male that has to spend time incubating may not be able to tolerate the reduction in manoeuvrability, and hence loss of efficiency at hunting, that a long tail, particularly if it is damaged, causes: with less time available for feeding, he cannot sacrifice hunting efficiency for the sake of a long tail.

Cuckoldry and guarding one's partner

Despite all the outward signs of monogamy and fidelity, Swallows are promiscuous at heart. Once their partners are preoccupied with incubating the eggs, males will make forays to neighbouring nests to copulate with other females. Such cuckoldry is quite common among apparently monogamous birds. In evolutionary terms, the most successful male is the one who passes on the most copies of his genes to the next generation. Consequently, males want to sire as many offspring as possible. Not satisfied with the three to six nestlings that their own partners can produce at a time, they try their luck elsewhere, copulating with other females whenever possible and leaving the cuckolded male and his partner to rear their young.

Females are not unwilling victims in this cuckoldry, and their interests do not always coincide with those of their own partners. Although they do not actively seek extra-marital mates, they are likely to have male suitors visiting them anyway. A female can reject a suitor if she wants to by attacking him or just flying away, but she may benefit from copulating with another male, especially if he has more desirable characteristics than her own partner, for example if he is more resistant to parasites. A young female that arrives back at the breeding grounds late in the season may find that the best males have already paired, and she may be left with a young, inferior partner. She may then get a better genetic father for some or all of her offspring by accepting a copulation with one of the males that has already paired up (each egg is fertilized separately, so a brood can be of mixed parentage). Having more than one genetic father for the nestlings in a brood may also spread the risk of these nestlings inheriting a characteristic that later turns out to be a disadvantage.

As happens when the female is choosing her partner for the season, she uses tail length as a guide to the suitability of philanderers as fathers for her offspring. She again prefers long-tailed, and also older, males on these occasions, and she is most likely to be dissatisfied with her own partner and accept another suitor if the former has a shorter tail than the latter. Even long-tailed males, however, are at risk of being cuckolded and females paired to them are willing to accept other good suitors. It is up to the male to spot and chase off such suitors. Naturally long-tailed males seem to be better at this: as Henrik Smith and his colleagues in Canada found, they manage to avoid being cuckolded, while shorter-tailed males do not.

Not all attempts at copulating outside the pair-bond may be successful, but we know from paternity studies such as DNA fingerprinting that some nestlings are not the genetic offspring of the males caring for them. Anders Møller found that in fifty families one-third of nestlings were unrelated to the male feeding them, and in the study by Henrik Smith and his colleagues ten illegitimate nestlings were detected in five out of eleven families studied. Two nests contained as many as three or four nestlings whose father was not the male paired with their mother.

This is bad news for the cuckolded male, of course. Not only does he fail to sire some or all of his partner's offspring, but he also ends up spending his valuable time and energy rearing someone else's. A male Swallow, therefore, tries to protect his interests. When his partner is fertile, that is when any copulations with her will fertilize any eggs developing inside her, he assiduously guards her, shadowing almost her every move, and preventing other males paying attention to her. This period of guarding need last only a fortnight or so for each clutch. The female is fertile from about five days before she lays the first egg until the day before she lays the last one, and it is during this time that another male could successfully fertilize some of her eggs. Her partner follows her around, keeping no more than a metre or two away and staying alert for the approach of a philandering male. The female at this time is usually busy finishing off the nest and collecting dry grass and feathers for the lining. Her partner accompanies her while she works but gives practically no help. If another male does approach, he vigorously sees him off. Guarding is particularly important where Swallows are nesting in groups, with many potential cuckolders, and also for early nesters, whose females are fertile when other males have the time to look for females with which to copulate.

Guarding is known to be effective at preventing extra-marital unions. In one experiment, Anders Møller removed some males for a few hours from a breeding site in his Danish population. He found that their unguarded females were chased more, and copulated with other males more, than females who still had males guarding them. Sometimes a male loses sight of his female through a lapse of attention or a necessary diversion to eat or drink, but he has a trick to stop her copulating surreptitiously with other males at such moments. He flies around the breeding site, giving an urgent alarm call as if he had spotted a predator. No such predator need exist but the effect is the same: the Swallows leave their nest sites and fly out into the open, thus curtailing any illicit copulating going on.

Guarding is not, however, just a selfish male ploy. Females are choosy and may not be interested in a suitor. At such a time, a female may actively encourage her partner to protect her from harassment by unwanted males especially when, for example, she is foraging for extra food and calcium-rich eggshells and grit for her developing eggs.

A male has to guard his female to protect his genetic interests, but he suffers as a result. Although he can feed at the same time as his partner, he probably cannot do so very efficiently. Because he follows her, he ends up feeding where she has already been. Any insects at the feeding site not eaten by the female are likely to be frightened off by her, leaving less for him. Consequently, males lose weight while guarding their females, and only good-quality males can successfully maintain a high level of guarding and keep other males away. Another disadvantage of guarding a female is that the male has no opportunity to copulate with other females himself. This extra-marital activity has to be left until his own partner has finished laying and is no longer fertile. Guarding can then be dispensed with and the male can spend time with other females while his partner incubates the eggs, an activity in which the European male plays no role, anyway.

Clearly, all this guarding is sometimes to no avail and another male does manage to sneak in and copulate with the female. The many nestlings that do not belong to the male in whose nest they hatch attest to this. Most successful illicit unions are with birds who have the opportunity to watch the activities of the pair. They know when a female is fertile and when her partner is not paying attention. If, for example, the latter is chasing off yet another interloper some distance from the nest, a male neighbour could visit and copulate with the unguarded female without being seen, at least until the deed is done.

A male can, however, act to minimize the effects of this cuckoldry. The first thing he can do if he knows or suspects that his partner has just copulated with another male is to copulate with her repeatedly himself to dilute his rival's sperm and increase the chances that he will still father the offspring. Even if he does not witness his female being unfaithful, he may see another male chasing her or may have lost contact with her. This may suggest that she was, or had the opportunity to be, involved in an extra-marital copulation, and he can act accordingly. In addition to repeated copulation, the male can later avoid wasting time and energy looking after nestlings that are unlikely to be his own. By spending more time feeding himself he might stay in better condition and improve his prospects of surviving until the following year, when he can try again. He probably cannot recognize his nestlings within a brood from those sired by another male, but if his suspicions were aroused during his partner's fertile period he can put less effort into caring for the brood as a whole. Anders Møller carried out an experiment to see if males did adjust their parental activities in this way. During the egg-laying stage, he caught males at night and released them in the morning when their partners had already been up for two hours. During this period, other males could and did copulate with these females. Since the detained males had lost contact with their partners, they would have been unsure whether the females' eggs laid in the next few days were theirs. Møller found that later on, during the nestling stage, the males who had been detained were more reluctant to give alarm calls and to come close to a potential predator (a stuffed Little Owl) than other males (who had also been caught at night but released before sunrise, so had no reason to suspect that their partners had been unfaithful); detained males also fed the nestlings less. This reduction in parental care by males who were probably uncertain of their paternity was apparent only in groups of Swallows; for pairs breeding alone, cuckoldry is unlikely, so the male may be more certain that he is the father. Similarly, males detained when their partners were incubating, and cuckoldry was not possible, also did not defend their nestlings less actively. It seems, therefore, that cuckolded males, or rather males who are not confident that they are the father, invest less in their partner's brood.

Egg-dumping

It is not only male Swallows that have doubts about whose children are in the nest. Female Swallows sometimes unwittingly look after eggs that are not their own. There are a few records of Cuckoos and cowbirds laying in Swallows' nests, but more often the foreign egg comes from another Swallow. Eggs laid by one female tend to look similar to each other and slightly different from those of another female. Despite this, Swallows cannot recognize their own eggs and an extra, odd-looking one goes unnoticed. Presumably, the risk of mistakenly removing one of their own eggs is too great for them to attempt to identify and remove an alien egg. Swallows lay only one egg a day but they cannot count either and appear unworried if two eggs turn up in the nest on the same day. However, they accept the extra eggs only if they appear during the normal egg-laying sequence or during incubation. A female is capable of ejecting any eggs that are laid in her nest before she has started laying herself.

The females 'dumping' eggs in this way are usually neighbours of the victimized female. In his Danish population, Anders Møller found that more than one in ten nests contained eggs of a female other than the nest-owner. The nests most at risk are those a few metres away from another nest when both are at the egg-laying stage. To see how frequent egg-dumping was at different stages of breeding, Møller put up nests of his own, some close to others and some with eggs in them; he found that old nests already containing eggs were the most likely to have eggs dumped in them. Guarding the nest is important to discourage egg-dumpers: nests very close to each other are less likely to suffer because each nest is effectively guarded by its neighbours as well as by its owners. A female can thus, to some extent, avoid having eggs dumped into her nest by choosing to breed near neighbours which are at a later stage of breeding, since they will be incubating or feeding nestlings while she is at the vulnerable egg-laying stage and will not be interested in egg-dumping. They will also unwittingly act as guards for her own nest against both egg-dumpers and infanticidal birds. The female will also benefit by having a desirable, good-quality male available as an extra-marital mating partner.

Dumping eggs in the nest of another female is a sensible strategy if the opportunity arises. It allows a female to produce more offspring than if she just laid a clutch in her own nest. A female who dumps eggs can both rear her own brood and have chicks in other nests with the hard work of rearing them being borne by other females: in Møller's study, such a female could be the mother of five fledglings on average, whereas the victims who looked after their eggs ended up with only three chicks of their own.

Living in groups

Swallows suffer many problems when they nest close to each other: more parasites; more threats to nestlings; more disagreements with neighbours; more cuckoldry and egg-dumping; and more competition for food. One of the worst problems is the higher incidence of debilitating parasites, such as blowfly larvae and fowl mites (see Chapter 6), which can mean that Swallows do not breed so successfully in large groups as they would by themselves. William Shields and Janice Crook in the Adirondacks found that those in large groups started nesting later and had smaller clutches than solitary pairs or those in small groups. They also hatched fewer eggs, reared fewer fledglings, and their nests more often failed completely. The main problem was blowfly larvae which plagued the nestlings. Not surprisingly, nestlings died from heavy infestations, particularly if the weather was cold, wet or windy making food scarce and lowering the nestlings' resistance. Infestation was more common in larger groups.

Similarly, in Anders Møller's Danish population, nests in large groups were more likely to be infested with fowl mites, which can also kill nestlings, and fewer chicks fledged in infested nests. Even parasites, such as the fowl mite, that are restricted to the nest may be transmitted between nests more easily in large groups, because the adults come into direct physical contact more often, when intruders visit nests, and during fights and extra-marital copulations.

Another major cause of death for nestlings is infanticide. This, too, was relatively more common in large groups in the Danish study, although not in the Adirondacks one. At the latter site, however, there were more losses of eggs in larger groups (some may have been due to other Swallows tossing them out). Egg-dumping was also more frequent in large groups in Denmark.

Individuals living in groups also suffer a number of social costs. Males are more likely to be cuckolded if they live in a group and have lots of neighbours, and so they have to spend more time guarding their partners and have less time for feeding. Females in groups are more likely to be harassed by ardent suitors. There are more unwelcome intruders at nests, intent on egg-dumping or destroying eggs or young nestlings, so more time has to be spent guarding the nest as well. This, however, conflicts with the male's desire to guard his partner more in groups, whether she is at the nest or away from it, and to do some cuckolding himself. Not surprisingly, therefore, Anders Møller found that females rather than males were most responsible for guarding the nest in large groups.

Competition over food may also be a problem in some large groups. Barbara Snapp found that, in a population in New York State, nestlings in groups of ten or more pairs weighed less than those of the same age in small groups suggesting that their parents were having more difficulty finding enough food. Anders Møller found that the more Swallows there were breeding at a site, the less food was available for each pair and the lower the frequency at which the nestlings were fed.

In terms of how successful pairs of Swallows are at rearing fledglings, those nesting in large groups sometimes do worse, or at least do no better, than solitary pairs or pairs nesting in small groups. The severity and the type of problems that Swallows face in large groups vary from site to site, and probably from year to year too but problems there clearly are, from high parasite infestations to a greater risk of being cuckolded. It may therefore seem that it is not worth Swallows nesting together. However, there are several possible reasons why Swallows are not always solitary.

One possibility put forward to explain group living by various species is that individuals forage more successfully by learning about good feeding sites from others. Rather than hunting for food by themselves, members of a group might be able to see where others are feeding and try their luck there. Alternatively, the nesting group might be a source of information about good feeding sites: if a Swallow returns to its nest with food, its neighbours, who may not know where food is, could follow it on its next trip to the source of that food. Such information gathering would be particularly important for a bird that feeds on ephemeral prey. A meadow may be buzzing with insects on a sunny morning but have none an hour later if it turns wet and windy. In such bad weather, the Swallows may have to go to another site, such as a windbreak, some distance away to find food. Even in good weather, a temporary swarm of mating flies or of mayflies emerging from a river may prove a bonanza of food. It would seem sensible to cash in on the knowledge of other birds that have found a good site.

Studies have shown, however, that Swallows do not follow each other on foraging trips, nor do they follow birds that have brought back food. They go out to feed by themselves or with their partner, and seem to catch as many insects when feeding alone as they do when feeding with others. Group feeding does not, therefore, bring any benefits.

Although Swallows cannot predict exactly where and when insects are going to be present, they probably have a good idea of which are the best feeding areas in different weather conditions: a river when it is wet, a clump of trees or a hedge in the wind. They usually feed close to the nest (see Chapter 3) so they are likely to know the local feeding sites well. So,

This nestling is troubled by mites. Severe infestations can kill.

although homing in on sites where they see others feeding may sometimes be useful, following other Swallows on feeding trips is unnecessary.

A second possible explanation of group living is that it provides defence against predation. A predator would be faced with more prey than it needs, so any one individual is less likely to be caught. In addition, many birds together may spot an approaching predator more easily, or mob it and chase it off more effectively if it comes close to the nests, and an aerial predator may find a swirling flock of birds confusing and be unable to single out one. On the debit side, however, a large group may be more conspicuous in the first place and may attract predators which look on it as a good supply of food, especially when newly fledged birds provide them with easy prey. In one instance in North America, a Bobcat destroyed the contents of 34 nests at a single site. Swallows do respond to a predator's presence sooner in large groups and more individuals join in mobbing it. The mobbing is not, however, a joint effort, and is most actively done by the pair whose nest is most threatened rather than by the group as a whole (see Chapter 6). Several studies have also found group living to have either no effect or an adverse effect on the level of predation of eggs, nestlings, fledglings and adults. In any case, predation on Swallows during the breeding season is not very common, so it is unlikely that they live in groups in order to reduce its effects.

There may not, of course, be any advantage to living in a group. Birds may aggregate just because resources such as nest sites or food are scarce and those that are available are clumped together. Barbara Snapp suggested that groups of Swallows form because the few available nest sites at a breeding site such as a farm are typically concentrated in one or a few outbuildings, forcing the birds to nest close to each other. This is not, however, always the case. Swallows do not spread themselves out over all the available sites and often apparently suitable sites for large groups are unused or are used by only one or few pairs. Sometimes, too, sites are used by solitary pairs in one year and by a group in another. So, Swallows are not compelled to nest together; they seem rather to gather where the resources are available. An abundance of food at a site allows a group to form, whereas there is no evidence that the clumped availability of nest sites forces Swallows into a group. The more insects there are around a nesting site, the larger the group that can be sustained. The amount of suitable feeding habitat, especially shelterbelts, which still provide a source of food in bad weather, is particularly important in determining the number nesting in a site.

Overall, it would seem advantageous for a pair of Swallows to nest by themselves. However, Anders Møller has suggested that certain individuals do derive some benefit from living in a group which may offset part of or all the costs. Although a male may be cuckolded and a female may have eggs dumped in her nest, there are also more opportunities for doing the cuckolding and the egg-dumping. Old males, who arrive at the nest site early, may benefit the most. They can get their own clutch started and then go off to copulate with other females and sire even more offspring, whereas young males are likely to be the ones who are cuckolded. Young females have the opportunity to copulate with the more desirable, older males in a group, so they may benefit from this. In addition, females can increase the number of eggs they lay by egg-dumping. For those males that fail to get a partner initially, the best option is to be with a group as they may still be able to acquire one later in the season, by killing a female's first brood and inducing a divorce or finding a widowed female. Overall, however, there are few benefits and many costs to living in a group.

William Shields and his colleagues at the State University of New York have put forward another reason why Swallows nest in groups. They suggested that Swallows are attracted to sites where other Swallows are already breeding because their presence indicates a good quality site. If an apparently suitable site does not already have Swallows, it may turn out to have a drawback. A cliff site may get flooded or damaged by rock falls, another site may be close to a bird of prey's nest, or at modern sites humans may remove nests from certain locations such as in garages that are being used. Such problems are unlikely to be evident at the time the male Swallow is prospecting for nest sites. However, if he chooses a place where other Swallows are nesting successfully then he is likely to be choosing a safe site, suitable for successful breeding.

Eventually, of course, a site will attract so many pairs that the effects of crowding, such as increased levels of parasite infestations, outweigh the advantages of choosing a safe site. Prospecting Swallows may then decide to go elsewhere, or resident Swallows who do not want more neighbours and all the problems they bring may chase them off. And, as Swallows start to fail to nest successfully because the group is too large, they in turn will move elsewhere.

6

BREEDING

'The swallow sweeps
The slimy pool, to build his hanging house
Intent.'
James Thomson

In Britain, the first Swallows are usually back at their nest sites and ready to lay their eggs early in May. Males are the first to arrive, before the females. First-year birds return later than older ones. The timing of laying varies from year to year, sometimes starting in April, but it may be delayed until late May and it is later in northern than in southern Britain. Elsewhere, there is also a north–south cline in both arrival dates and when laying starts, with Swallows in southern Spain and northern Africa laying in March, while North European birds do not lay until late May or June.

The reason for differences in arrival and laying dates between areas and between years lies in the weather and its effect on the Swallow's food supply. As temperatures rise, there is a resurgence of insect life in spring from practically nothing in winter, but the timing varies. A sunny spell at the end of April means plenty of food for Swallows; a sprinkling of snow means hardly any at all. In addition, numbers of the large flies favoured by Swallows (see Chapter 3) start to swell a little later than those of small insects. Swallows arrive in Britain in April and May to take advantage of this. The first usually arrive in the south in early April followed by mass arrivals over the next few weeks. They gradually move up the country as the weather improves, reaching northern areas by early May. The northward movement in Europe at first follows closely the 8.9°C (48°F) isotherm, but after mid-April the Swallows arrive at northerly sites, where the temperatures are even lower but the food supply is presumably still adequate. Laying then starts when large insects are becoming abundant.

Laying is timed to coincide with improving weather conditions and food supply, but the early stages of breeding are probably not difficult ones for the Swallow. Insects are rich sources of the protein, fats and energy that the female needs to produce eggs. Sally Ward measured daily energy requirements of 112 kilojoules for female Swallows at Stirling at this time, an amount a female can easily get in a day during the egg-laying period unless the weather is continuously cold and wet, and even then the female's fat reserves act as an extra fuel supply. Getting enough calcium for her eggs is potentially more of a problem during the laying period, but to get this nutrient she eats snail shells, grit and pieces of eggshell, which are rich in it. When the weather is very bad, however, the female may take two days rather than one to produce an egg, or lay a small egg, or just stop laying altogether.

A more problematic period for the European Swallow is the incubation stage. Although the female's daily energy requirements are slightly lower (at 105 kilojoules) during incubation than when she was laying eggs, because she incubates by herself, and because the time she has free to forage is thus restricted by the need to stay on the nest to keep the eggs warm, she could face real difficulties in getting enough food. She therefore waits until she can avoid the worst of the bad weather in the spring. In Stirling, the weather usually improved considerably during May, allowing the Swallows to lay and incubate their clutches in the second half of the month with relatively little risk of their food supply failing.

Nest sites

Old sites and old nests are often re-used year after year, although not necessarily by the same birds. An old nest may just need a bit of extra mud to bolster a crumbling rim and a fresh lining of feathers added before it is serviceable again. After several years a nest may become quite large and robust in this way. Some nests last ten to fifteen years and one is known to have lasted 48 years, but the average is about seven years.

There are both advantages and disadvantages to using an old nest. Re-using one obviously saves time and energy spent collecting mud and making the nest. An old nest can be repaired in as little as a tenth of the time it takes to make a new one. This is important because an early start

Nests may be built on top of a beam or other support, or on a vertical surface.

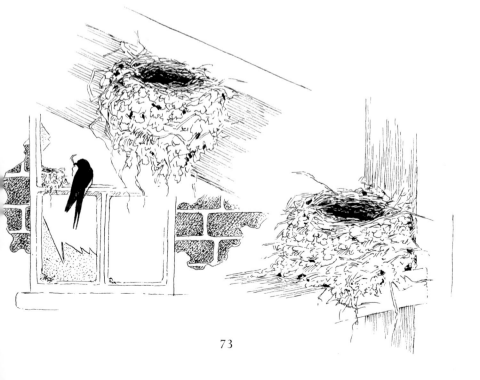

to breeding increases the chances a pair has of fledging two or even three broods successfully. In addition, a nest already present at a site is likely to be in the best position, safe from the wind and the rain and from predators. If a Swallow re-uses a nest in which it bred successfully in the previous year, then it knows that the nest has no obvious problems associated with it. A new nest, on the other hand, may have to be built in a less favourable place or in one that may have drawbacks in the future. For example, its support may be weak and it may fall down, or it may be flooded later in the year, something about which the Swallow would not know at the time he selected the nest site. If a pair decides to build a new nest, the birds also run the risk of being caught by predators when they are collecting mud on the ground. However, old nests have disadvantages, too. They harbour parasites from the previous year, which can harm both adults and chicks. In addition, old nests eventually become unstable: they may fall under the weight of yet another brood, smashing eggs and crushing chicks. Falling nests can sometimes be a significant cause of mortality.

Whether a Swallow chooses to use an old nest may vary from place to place and from year to year. If more than one old nest is available at a site, a Swallow may be able to avoid parasites by using a different nest in alternate years; most parasites will die if they are deprived of a host for a year. On the other hand, if food is abundant early on and local conditions favour a long breeding season, a pair may choose to build a new nest to avoid parasites and still have time to rear two broods. The proportion of birds building a new nest varies from year to year and from site to site, but typically as many as six to nine out of every ten pairs re-use a nest rather than build a new one. Those Swallows that do re-use a nest are generally those that have successfully reared a brood in it previously. Those that lose a brood often move to another nest or build a new one rather than use a nest that has proved unsuitable.

Early arrivals at the breeding site, the experienced birds, generally re-use nests, spending just a few days on repairs before laying their eggs. Later birds, often those in their first year of breeding, may not arrive until the old nests at a site that are still usable have been appropriated, or if the available nests are at a crowded site they may encounter aggression and interference from neighbours; they then have no choice but to make a new one if they decide to stay at that site. This can take a week or more, and these birds end up laying late, perhaps not until June. They consequently have time to rear only one brood during the summer, whereas the early birds can fit in two or three.

The same nest is often used for the first, second and third broods. In a German study, for example, 84 per cent of pairs, and in a Belgian one 90 per cent of pairs, used the same nest. In one case, a pair started a second brood while still feeding a first brood in another nest; they went on to have a third brood that season! The proportion moving or building a new nest, however, varies from year to year and from site to site. In a study in the Adirondacks in New York State, only just over half the pairs re-used nests for a second brood; those which had had a successful first brood were more likely to change nests than those which had failed,

The nest is built up from pellets of mud, put into place with the bill.

perhaps because parasite numbers had increased in the nests that had contained nestlings (see below).

When a new nest is built, it is usually attached to a horizontal support such as a window, a chimney ledge or a wooden beam in a barn, especially in a corner where two sides of the nest can be supported. A projection such as a nail or hook in a wall can be sufficient to start a nest off. A few nests are built straight on to a vertical surface, but such unsupported nests are more likely to fall down. In a study in Scotland, Derek McGinn and Hugh Clark noted that four out of five nests were built on a beam or in a roof apex. Most nests are placed 2 – 6 m above the ground, the average in the same Scottish study being 3.3 m. They are usually placed 10 – 15 cm below a ceiling or overhang to provide both protection from the weather and predators and a warm stable environmental temperature for the brood.

Occasionally, separate objects are used as a base for a nest; these have included a shoebox, a shrimp pot, a hat hanging on a wall, a car-window frame hanging in a garage, a picture frame, a chain on a wall, a pulley, a sunflower seed head nailed to a beam in a barn, hanging lamps and light bulbs, lamp shades and brackets, and old Swallows' nests. The most unusual site was perhaps the corpse of an owl, hanging from a rafter in a barn. There are also records of Swallows building their nests on those of raptors and wasps. Most nests are built above ground level, but occasionally Swallows go underground and nest in a well or abandoned mine, or bunker. In addition, there are some instances of Swallows using moving trains or boats as nest sites, building the nest, incubating and rearing the nestlings despite the lack of a stationary substrate. At one site, Lake George in New York State, successive pairs of Swallows nested beneath the guard rails of a steamer for over 50 years.

Swallows are relatively tolerant of having their nest moved, especially when they have nestlings to feed. If a nest falls at this time, it is possible to transfer the nestlings to a substitute nest such as a box, placed nearby, and the parents will quickly adapt to the new nest and site. Biologists at Cornell University even managed to move two Swallow nests to a new site 3.5 km away by transporting them on a vehicle very slowly; the trip took 27 hours of daylight for one nest and thirteen hours for the other, with the Swallows continuing to feed the nestlings. Swallows return to the previous location of a nest and are initially confused if it has moved, even if to a human observer it appears to be still in view, but by flying around the site they soon find the new location. If the nest is on a moving object, the Swallows come to associate the nest with the vehicle rather than with the last location of the nest and they fly direct to the vehicle.

There have been attempts to provide artificial nest sites for Swallows, ranging from just nailing up a narrow wooden platform at a suitable site in or on a building, to act as a support for a nest, to putting up complete artificial nests or relocating real abandoned ones. These have had some success. In one attempt in France, for example, Swallows laid in two out of seven nests made of papier mâché and four out of nine made of clay mixed with twigs, which were put up under a bridge. The main difficulty in attracting Swallows to breed, however, is that they are traditional in the sites they use and they are unlikely to use a new site unless there is already an active Swallow's nest present. Once a breeding site has become established, more young birds are likely to be attracted to it and to build their own nests there.

In some areas, particularly in North America, eaves of buildings, bridges, culverts, open barns or wharves are popular sites for nests. Unlike House Martins, however, Swallows in Europe rarely put their nests in such exposed places. They generally prefer the interior of buildings, somewhere relatively secluded, high up and dark, quiet and protected from predators and the elements. The enclosed nest of a House Martin, in contrast to a Swallow's open one, has its own built-in protection and can be safely placed outside. Indoor sites probably resemble the original cave nesting sites of Swallows. The white feathers used to line the nest, the dark-spotted white eggs, and the pale yellow edges to the bill of the nestling may help the parents find the nest in the dark.

Whether inside or outside, the birds need a good approach path to the nest site. They are not, however, put off by closed doors and windows and can enter buildings by surprisingly small holes, just a couple of inches across. The nest is often placed near a door or window to allow the parents easy and rapid access and egress. Provided the nest itself is safely sited, the parents are generally not worried by the comings and goings of humans or other animals around them and will even nest in occupied rooms. At Stirling, Swallows regularly used to nest on a ledge between a kirk and the adjacent manse, ignoring all the churchgoers passing to and fro just a metre or two away while sitting on the eggs or feeding the nestlings.

Nests are often situated inside buildings where livestock such as pigs, cattle or horses are kept, the Swallows perhaps benefiting from the extra warmth early in the season, as well as the flies associated with the animals. In Anders Møller's study in Denmark, most Swallows bred in cow sheds when there were few Swallows using the area, whereas when the number of pairs increased, and they were competing for nest sites, relatively more of them had to use pig sheds.

Why Swallows in Europe are such confirmed indoor nesters compared with those in North America is not clear. There may be an element of competition with House Martins. There are a few records of one species destroying or taking over the nests of the other, and the presence of House Martin nests on the best sites on the outside of buildings may put off Swallows from trying to build there. Nevertheless, in North America, Swallows nest side by side with Cliff Swallows on the outside of human-made structures, so competition for nest sites cannot be the whole story. Alternatively, suitable indoor sites may be less available in some areas than outdoor ones such as large open barns and bridges. Henrik Smith and Robert Montgomerie suggest that the reason for the difference in choice of nest site between North American and European Swallows may lie in the longer period of association between the latter race and humans.

Nest-building

The nest is cup-shaped, usually a quarter to a half of a sphere and measuring about 20 x 10 cm, new ones being shallower than old, rebuilt ones. The shape depends on where the nest is situated. One built against a vertical surface is usually a half-circle at the top and more pointed towards

A Swallow collects a pellet of mud in its bill.

the bottom, whereas one built on a horizontal surface is likely to be more circular and shallower, with a flatter bottom. Nests in corners have walls built up to fill the spaces.

Mud pellets mixed with organic matter, especially dry grass and horsehair, are used to construct the nest, which is then lined with dry grass and feathers, usually white ones. The nest can contain up to 1400 pellets of mud, although half that is sufficient. One nest, when taken to pieces, was found to contain 7.5 oz (213 g) of dried earth, 1635 rootlets, 139 white pine needles, 450 pieces of dried grass, ten chicken feathers, four pieces of wood, two human hairs and some pieces of leaf and cotton as well as a tablespoon of tiny pieces of rootlets and grass. An analysis of nests of Swallows in Montana found that the birds used mainly loam and sandy loam rather than clay soil. Our knowledge of other building materials suggests that the relative proportions of sand and clay used will affect how well the mud pellets stick together and to the substrate, how strong the mud structure will be, how easy the mud is to manipulate, and how much it will shrink as it dries or swell when it gets wet. A high sand content decreases the strength of the dried mud, as does the addition of vegetation and hair. On the other hand, sand makes the mud easier to work and both the sand and the organic matter reduce the amount by which the nest contracts and expands in relation to temperature and moisture content. The grass and hair also help to bind the mud pellets together and prevent cracks spreading.

The type of material used for the nest is probably a compromise, so that the final nest is reasonably strong and stays up for at least one breeding season while the mud is still easy to manipulate and will not shrink or expand excessively. Swallows have a fairly easy nest to build as it is just an open cup. It is more difficult for some other swallows and martins, which build an enclosed nest with or without an entrance tunnel. The Cliff Swallow of North America, for example, uses more sand than the Swallow, probably because it needs mud that is more easily worked for its particular nest design, but in doing so it sacrifices strength, and its nests are more fragile than those of the Swallow.

When mud and grass are scarce, however, Swallows will use substitutes. They have been recorded using seaweed and algae to patch up old nests or to build new ones. In addition, other soft material such as rootlets, pine needles, fragments of wood, cotton thread and human hair may be mixed in with the mud. Occasionally, a nest of another bird or a narrow hole in a wall or roof or a natural niche in a rock is appropriated and little or no mud need be used as a foundation; just some organic material such as straw, dry grass and feathers is sufficient for a nest in these circumstances. One nest was in the cup of a ceiling fan, when it was not in use, and again included very little mud.

Both sexes are involved in the building work, but the female often does more than the male. Each spends a couple of hours, mostly in the morning, working on the nest; the afternoon is spent feeding, probably to build up fat reserves to last the night. At the peak of building, I recorded pairs at Stirling making 20 or 25 trips in one hour to collect mud, although eight

Dry grass is collected to help bind the mud pellets of the nest together.

or nine times an hour was more usual. For one nest it was calculated that the birds made 100 trips a day each, travelling in all 137 miles (219 km) and working a total of six hours. It takes a week to ten days to build a nest but bad weather can slow the birds down, as they have to spend more of their time searching for food instead of building. Work can then be delayed by several days. Dry weather, when mud is unavailable, also prevents the birds working. Mud is collected from nearby, usually just 10 – 30 m away. The banks of a stream or pond are often used but a damp patch of mud on a dirt road is sufficient.

A Swallow collects mud by pushing its bill into it and so gathering a small piece at a time in the bill to take to the site for the nest, where it is pushed into place, again with the bill. The first pellets go to make the floor, if the nest is started on a beam or ledge and then the walls are gradually built up. New pellets are placed over those already there, like bricks in a wall, and strands of hair or grass are used to help bind the mud. When the nest is built against a vertical surface, the birds start by making a support of mud which will form the bottom of the nest. The walls are then built up first along the vertical surface on each side of the projection of mud and then extended outwards and curved until the two sides meet.

The shape and structure of a nest is important in several respects. It must keep the eggs and nestlings warm, but not too warm, it must give them room to grow, and it must last long enough for them to fledge successfully. The placing of the nest just below the ceiling of a building helps to maintain a warm and stable temperature, buffering it from the extremes of temperatures outside, especially in buildings housing animals. Anders Møller recorded temperatures of 18 – 29°C at ceiling height compared with a range of 6 – 23°C outdoors. This high, stable temperature is important, because the female alone has to keep the eggs and young chicks warm. This task is easier, and she can use less energy, if the eggs and chicks do not cool rapidly while she is away feeding. Later in the season, however, when the nestlings are large and fill the nest cup the problem is one of heat stress and dehydration rather than chilling.

Early in the season active nests are large, robust structures. They are built by old, experienced birds and are roomy enough for a large clutch. Young, inexperienced birds arriving later in the season build shallower nests. Second-clutch nests are also shallower and wider. There are two main reasons for this. First-year birds, and older birds laying a second time that season, may have slightly smaller clutches, so they do not need large nests; and, secondly, the weather is warmer in midsummer so the eggs and chicks do not need the insulation provided by a thick nest cup.

The lining of grass and feathers is completed in a few days. The preferred feathers are small, white poultry feathers, which appear to be so desirable that Swallows will fight over them. If coloured feathers are added to the nest, the Swallow is likely to throw them out. Where feathers are scarce or absent a substitute such as sheep's wool is used. About 20 – 40 feathers are added to the lining, until the time the female starts incubating. More are added the larger the clutch is. At this stage, and when the newly hatched chicks need to be kept warm as well, the feathers insulate the nest and help prevent the eggs or chicks losing heat rapidly when the female is absent. The female starts throwing out some of the feathers when the nestlings are about six to ten days old until only a few are left by the time they are ready to fledge. At this stage the nestlings can keep themselves warm, and it is possible that they may overheat and dehydrate if there are a lot of feathers in the nest. Fewer feathers are used for the second clutch, perhaps because the weather is warmer then.

The importance of the feather lining for insulating the eggs and chicks is clearly seen if feathers are removed from nests. Anders Møller showed that, at nests with only a few feathers left in them, the female has to spend longer periods on the eggs and stays away for shorter periods because the eggs cool more quickly without the insulating feather layer. The nestlings from such nests are also affected: they weigh less at fifteen days old and take a day or so longer to fledge.

White feathers are gathered for the nest lining.

Eggs and clutch size

Once the nest is lined, the female starts to lay her eggs, one a day, early in the morning. The eggs are smooth, glossy and elongated elliptical or oval. The ground colour is white and this is spotted with red-brown and some lilac-grey. The eggs measure 19.7 x 13.6 mm on average (range 16.7 – 23.0 x 12.3 – 14.8 mm) and weigh 1.9 g (range 1.4 – 2.1 g). There is some geographical variation, with those in North America measuring 18.8 x 13.5 mm and those of the race *gutturalis* measuring 18.9 x 13.3 mm.

The clutch size is usually three to six but typically more than 80 per cent of clutches contain four or five eggs and only a few per cent two eggs at one extreme or seven or eight eggs at the other. Larger clutches have been recorded but may contain eggs from more than one female or eggs from two separate laying attempts. In Britain, clutches of four or five are usual (mean 4.4). Clutches are slightly larger in the north than in the south of Britain. There is also a seasonal decline, due partly to small second and third clutches and partly to late breeders having a single small clutch. Derek McGinn and Hugh Clark, for example, recorded a mean clutch size in Scotland of 5.02 in May and 4.08 in August. This reduction is probably related to the shorter daylight available for feeding nestlings as the season progresses; in addition, late breeders may not have the physical qualities required to produce and rear a large brood. Elsewhere, clutch size is similar, often four or five, and varies little geographically.

In Europe as a whole, second clutches increase slightly in size with latitude and become less frequent. Second clutches are also often slightly smaller than first ones, and third clutches even smaller than second ones. In Florentino de Lope's study in Extremadura, Spain, for example, where third clutches are quite frequent, mean sizes were 4.99 for first clutches, 4.52 for second clutches and 3.89 for third clutches, and in Karl-Heinz Loske's study in central Westphalia the mean sizes were 4.59, 4.36 and 4.0 for first, second and third clutches, respectively.

Incubation

During the egg-laying period, the female spends progressively more time on the eggs, perhaps warming them a little, especially at night. The first-laid eggs may therefore start developing a little before the last are laid. Incubation does not start in earnest, however, until the last egg is in the nest. Only the female incubates the eggs, at least in the European race; there are reports of males on the eggs, but these are rare. The female has a brood-patch, an area of bare, highly vascularized skin on her belly through which she passes body heat to the eggs and, later, to the nestlings. The male does not have a brood-patch so cannot warm the eggs so effectively. He does very occasionally, however, sit on the eggs or stand over them for a minute or so. I have twice seen males doing this, but in general they take little interest. Once, when I had caught an incubating female, her mate returned to the nest in her absence, peered at the eggs but made no attempt to sit on them, left, and returned a little later with another female!

In the North American race of the Swallow, in contrast, the male does help with the incubation, taking turns with the female. During the day, in mild weather, he can keep the eggs as warm as his partner can. Because the eggs are not left uncovered so much their temperature does not drop, and so the male primarily has only to keep them at the same temperature rather than warming them, although he can increase their temperature if they have cooled. He does only a small proportion of the incubation, however. Gregory Ball recorded male Swallows in New Jersey incubating for about 12 per cent of the time against the female's 70 per cent, while in Henrik Smith and Robert Montgomerie's study in Ontario the males were on the eggs for only 9 per cent of the daytime period of incubation. The Ontario males incubated for shorter periods than their partners and began fewer incubation periods per hour. A North American male seems to be most helpful when his partner needs to spend more time feeding herself – when temperatures are low, early in the day and late in the incubation period – but he cannot compensate completely for the female; if she disappears, he seems unable or unwilling to incubate the clutch himself.

Smith and Montgomerie suggest that North American males help with the incubation duties because their nests are more exposed to the weather, making it difficult for the female to incubate by herself. Because nests in North America are often built on the outside of human-made structures, they may be colder than those of the European Swallow, which are usually well protected inside a building from the inconstancies of the climate.

Typically, the European female sits on the eggs for periods of 10 – 20 minutes, longer in cold weather than in warm weather, and longer early and late in the day when the temperature is low. When she has to leave them to forage, she stays away for only a short time, usually two to seven minutes. She also spends less time away as the day of hatching approaches. Over the day, the female spends an average of 70 – 80 per cent of her time incubating. The rest of the time is spent feeding, although, if the weather is very warm, she sometimes leaves the nest just to perch nearby. There have been reports of the male feeding the female while she is on the nest, but this is probably very rare behaviour; I have never seen it myself.

The temperature of the eggs drops rapidly by several degrees when the female is off the nest, so, to maintain their temperature, at about 36°C, she has to keep her periods of feeding as short as possible. This can be a problem in cold weather when food is scarce and the birds take longer to find enough to satisfy their hunger; if the weather is persistently bad over several days, the female may be forced to desert and start another clutch later. At Stirling, females would leave the eggs for only five minutes or so in warm weather but in cold weather they would be away for eight minutes on average and sometimes much longer. In my first year at Stirling, one day at the beginning of June was very cold – there were even some flurries of snow – and the Swallows spent only a third of their time during the day incubating their eggs. They would snuggle down into the nest with feathers plumped out and stay there for 20 – 30 minutes; then they would slip away to search for food, abandoning their clutches for two

Newly hatched chicks are blind and almost naked – the feathers in the nest help to keep them warm.

or three hours at a time. Nils–Jarle Ytreberg recorded similar changes in incubation behaviour in Norway on a day when the weather was severe. Three females incubated for only 27 per cent, 31 per cent and 50 per cent of the time, compared with 70 – 79 per cent before the bad weather; they deserted the eggs for 7 – 12 hours. The egg temperatures dropped to about 10°. In all these cases, however, the bad weather lasted only a day and the clutches hatched successfully.

During incubation, females maintain large reserves of fuel in the form of fat, and can be some 2 g heavier than their partners. These reserves buffer them against the vagaries of the weather, as the following example shows. At Stirling, Gareth Jones weighed females during incubation by placing the nest on a balance and recording the additional weights of the parents at the nest. One incubating female lost 9 per cent of her weight over six hours of continuously cold and wet weather. The same female's weight dropped from 22.7 g on the eighth day of incubation to 19.8 g on the twelfth day, and she changed from incubating for 63 per cent of the time to only 8.7 per cent; and twice she left the eggs for longer than two hours. She was probably on the point of deserting the clutch. Fortunately, the weather improved on the next day and the female regained her former weight. Besides being an important insurance against bad weather, fat reserves in an incubating female also probably provide a long-term source of fuel to be used later on when the young nestlings have to be brooded, allowing her to catch food for her offspring rather than for herself. In addition, if she loses her clutch she is still in a good enough condition to be able to lay another one quickly.

Rearing the young

It usually takes fifteen days for the eggs to hatch, and they do so within a day or two of each other. The female sometimes helps the nestlings to prise themselves out. Afterwards, she picks up the broken pieces of eggshell and drops them over the side. At first, the nestlings are not the prettiest of creatures; they are pink and naked, with only a few tufts of grey down on the back and the large head, and their bulging eyes are shut. They lie flat on the bottom of the nest, feebly raising their heads when their parents come to feed them. The down probably helps trap warm air in the bottom of the nest and stops the chicks cooling down rapidly when the female is absent. A second coat of short down grows between the sprouting feathers in the second week. The nestling's feathers usually cut through the skin at five or six days, sometimes earlier, while the feather tips sprout at eight to ten days. The eyes open at between four and nine days, first as a slit and then gradually until they are fully open. By twelve days the chicks at last look like real Swallows, albeit rather dishevelled, dull-coloured ones, with stubby wings and tail.

For the first few days the naked nestlings cannot generate their own body heat, and the female must brood them. She gradually spends less time on the nest and more time collecting food as the nestlings rapidly grow and they become more able to maintain a high body temperature. They do not need high levels of brooding after they are about seven or eight days old. Nestlings can partially regulate their own body temperature at this age. The female may, however, brood them for part of the time up to ten to fourteen days of age, especially in cool weather. A nestling only seven or eight days old with the body feathers just sprouting has very poor

Once their feathers have grown, nestlings look almost like adults, but with a stubby tail.

insulation; its feathers provide much better insulation by the time it is fifteen days old. At about this age it can regulate its own temperature quite well so does not need its mother to provide warmth, but the female may still brood nestlings up to the time of fledging if there is a risk of them being chilled. She also broods them at night until they are about ten to fourteen days old, when she starts roosting by the nest. The male, in contrast, does not help brood the nestlings but feeds them from the time they hatch. Males have, however, been reported to help with the brooding, and North American males regularly do so, in one study brooding for about 13 per cent of the time, against the female's 47 per cent.

At about the time of hatching, a nestling weighs 1.5 – 1.9 g. It grows rapidly, especially between the fourth and tenth days, putting on 2 – 2.5 g a day and is heaviest when about fifteen days old. This peak weight is variable but usually averages 22 – 25 g. After the peak, it declines steadily until the chick fledges, owing to loss of water from the maturing tissues. The average weight at fledging is 19 or 20 g. Nestlings put on fat as they grow – a valuable source of energy used to cushion them from the effects of bad weather when food may be short.

About three or four days after hatching, the nestlings are strong enough to beg whenever their parents approach the nest. The inside of the nestling's mouth is a conspicuous bright yellow, and the gape flanges are pale yellow: unmistakable targets for parents returning with food in the gloom of a barn. The nestlings vie with each other for the adult's attention; they stretch forwards, bills open wide, and call noisily as their mother or father alights at the nest. A Roman writer in the third century claimed that 'The mother Swallow accustoms her young to the idea of justice by impartial distribution of food, training them to observe the law of equality'; but, in reality, no such high principles exist. Siblings behave selfishly; each wants to look after itself, and the most demanding are given the food.

How often the nestlings are fed depends on a number of factors, principally on how many are in the brood and how old they are. Feeding rates do not increase linearly with the size of the brood, however, so each nestling in a large brood is fed a little less often than one in a small brood. Young nestlings are fed only a few times an hour; the rate increases as the nestlings grow and peaks when they are about thirteen days old. The nestlings are fed less frequently as they approach fledging: perhaps an attempt by parents to lure them out.

The parents feed the brood for most of the available daylight hours, but they do so most frequently late in the morning. They usually leave their roost site just before sunrise but on cold mornings when insects are not flying they may leave two or three hours later. At Stirling, each parent fed half-grown nestlings in first broods of four or five about twenty times an hour late in the morning, but only about eight times an hour first thing in the morning. The feeding rate continued high in the afternoon but tailed off in the evening to about ten times an hour; the parents would go to roost shortly after sunset. In contrast, in cold, wet and windy weather, the parents managed to bring only a few feeds an hour. On an average day, however, between them they would collect some 400 loads of food in all.

85

Nestlings beg noisily when a parent approaches, but only one gets the meal.

When the nestlings are a few days old, and the female is occupied with brooding them, the male is the main provider, but later he often feeds less frequently than the female. This does vary between broods: sometimes males bring as many as or even more feeds than females. Second broods are fed more frequently, but the parents have fewer daylight hours in which to collect the food and the meals they bring are smaller (see Chapter 3), so second-brood nestlings are not fed more than their earlier siblings.

Both parents tidy up after their offspring, swallowing or carrying away all their droppings for the first few days after hatching. The droppings are enclosed in a gelatinous membrane (known as a faecal sac), so it is easy for the parents to dispose of them. The adults carry them in the bill and drop them some way, usually 5 – 25 m, from the nest. They sometimes peck at the vents of the nestlings in order to stimulate them to defecate. The nestlings begin to defecate out of the nest by themselves after five or six days, or at least orient themselves so that the droppings are deposited at the rim of the nest ready for the parents to pick up. Most droppings are disposed of in this way by the ninth to the fourteenth day, but the parents continue to remove some faecal sacs if they are present.

Leaving the nest

The young Swallows leave the nest when they are about 18 – 23 days old, the whole brood taking a couple of days to fledge. The parents lure them out by uttering a contact call (see Chapter 4) and by not going immediately to the nest to feed them. They may hover in front of the nest for a while, leave, and then return to repeat the performance enticing the nestlings to take their first flight. Initially the fledglings do not venture far, perhaps just edging out to perch near the nest rather than launching into full flight.

The parents deposit them in a safe place, such as a branch on a tree, while they go hunting, returning to feed them. The young Swallows beg noisily when their parents return and sometimes fly up to them to take the food on the wing. They are fed for another week or so. Most fledglings can feed themselves after six to eight days, but they may remain near the nest with their parents for longer, usually three to four weeks; one family stayed together for two-and a-half months. Family ties may be maintained during migration: migrating Swallows have been seen feeding juveniles in flight. However, first-brood fledglings may be evicted from the site by their father if he and his partner are starting a second clutch.

If fledglings do stay around, they spend much of their time just loafing around the nest site, often on wires. Although play is not an important activity for young Swallows, they do sometimes play, most often engaging in some sort of nest-building activity, such as picking up a beakful of mud or collecting feathers. In one report, three juveniles were seen repeatedly dropping and catching a white feather in flight. Adults also occasionally engage in similar behaviour with feathers.

Defending the young

In addition to bringing them food, the parents have to protect their offspring from danger. Few predators can reach the nest apart from specialist climbers such as rats and weasels, but fledglings are particularly

Parents keep the nest tidy by removing the chicks' droppings.

vulnerable to cats and raptors. Small nestlings gape silently if they are disturbed, while older nestlings and incubating or brooding females usually keep their heads down in the nest and remain silent at any sign of danger and when they hear an alarm call. If the predator comes up to the nest, the parent's response varies: it may just slip away quietly or after uttering a few alarm calls, or it may stay near the nest, or even fly towards the predator, calling continuously. Swallows outside the nest which are looking after themselves alone may simply fly out of the path of an approaching predator or even land on the ground to evade an aerial one, but a direct threat at the nest is more likely to be tackled head-on.

A conspicuous feature of sites where a group of Swallows is breeding is their joint mobbing activity when a predator appears. They respond quickly to any threat by attacking. Swallows will mob by themselves but they also do it in groups, and the more nests there are at a site the more birds are available to mob. Adults outside the nest persistently pursue and dive at potential predators such as cats, dogs, weasels, squirrels, humans and birds of prey such as Kestrels and Sparrowhawks in an effort to drive them away. They utter a noisy two-syllable alarm call, 'zi-wit', especially when they approach the predator during a dive. At times they even hit it as they swoop past and they also sometimes hover over the predator and buffet it with their wings. They keep circling or swooping in a figure-of-eight pattern until the danger has gone.

Mobbing is a dangerous activity for the mobber: the predator naturally turns its attention to the bird noisily calling out and dive-bombing it, and sometimes manages to catch it. There are records of Swallows being caught by a Magpie, Sparrowhawks and cats when they have come too close. The risk is relatively small, but it is a real one. Why do so many Swallows at a

Swallows aggressively mob and chase off predators.

Fledglings often fly up to an approaching parent to be fed.

breeding site turn out to mob a predator and risk their lives? Are they, as it appears, combining their defences to get rid of the predator so that the whole group benefits, or is each bird looking after its own interests?

William Shields has studied the mobbing behaviour of Swallows in the Adirondacks, New York State, to see which of these possibilities is most likely. He noted that several features of Swallow mobbing suggest that the adults do it to protect their own, and only their own, offspring. More individuals take part, and they are bolder, calling and coming close to the predator, when nestlings are being reared than at other times. In addition, mobbing is more intense when the predator is close to a nest with eggs or nestlings. Swallows that are not yet parents join in, but the parents whose own nest is threatened are most likely to mob the predator. The others in the mobbing group are usually near neighbours of the threatened pair, so they would perceive the predator as a danger to their own nest as well.

Rather than co-operating to mob as a group, many individuals just cash in on the mobbing activity of others. While the parents whose own eggs or nestlings are directly threatened will do risky things such as uttering alarm calls and diving at the predator, others, including near neighbours, will merely fly in circles over the predator, keeping quiet and refraining from swooping too close. In this way they can find out what the predator is and whether it is approaching their own nest, without putting themselves in danger. Other birds will just perch nearby and watch. The mobbing is basically a selfish behaviour, designed to protect the nest of the bird doing it. Swallows act in their own interests, not those of others in the group.

Both members of a pair usually co-operate in mobbing. In his Danish population, Anders Møller found that females appear to be bolder when they encounter a predator at the nest than are males, and are more likely to call out in alarm and to fly towards it. Females also become more likely

Newly fledged Swallows stay close to the nest at first.

to attack a predator once they have started egg-laying and incubation, whereas their partners do not. Both parents, however, respond with attack rather than evasion when they have nestlings, especially when they are ready to fledge. Birds breeding in groups respond more boldly than those nesting by themselves, while yearling birds are more reluctant to attack than older ones. The differences between birds and at different stages of nesting may reflect the value of the eggs or nestlings to the parents. If a predator takes a clutch of eggs early in the season, for example, the parents still have time to lay another one or two successfully, whereas they may be unable to do so if they lose nestlings later on; they may, therefore, be more willing to take risks to defend the latter. Similarly, yearlings will probably be alive to breed in the following year if they lose a brood, whereas an older bird may not see another summer. In addition, how much effort male Swallows put into defence seems to depend on how certain they are that the eggs or nestlings are actually their own, being less willing to do anything risky if they are likely to have been cuckolded (see Chapter 5).

In contrast to the European Swallow, males of the North American race in William Shields' study mobbed more intensely than females, especially at the nestling stage. Shields suggested that males are more persistent mobbers because they are protecting their partners as well as their offspring. At his study site, as is often the case elsewhere, it is more difficult for a male to find a partner than for a female. There are usually plenty of males present but not enough females to go around, and some males do not manage to get a partner at all (see Chapter 5). So a male does not want to lose his partner; he is willing to risk his own life to protect her as well as to protect his offspring. A female, on the other hand, is interested primarily in her offspring; if her partner dies, she will find another one. So, she mobs to protect her eggs and especially her nestlings, rather than to protect her partner. The difference between European and North American birds may be that the latter are less promiscuous; as the North American male helps the female to incubate the eggs, he has less time for philandering. If he is more certain that he is the father of the eggs or nestlings in the nest, he may be more prepared to risk his life defending them.

Unpaired or recently widowed males also sometimes take risks and dive-bomb predators. Their main interest may also be in protecting females. An unpaired male sometimes helps a paired female in the hope that she will mate with him at a future date. In addition, males other than the nest-owner may have already fathered some of the nestlings in a nest (see Chapter 5) and are therefore willing to defend them by mobbing a predator.

Mobbing is seen not only in response to a direct threat to the nest. Swallows will also harass potential predators when away from the nest, even outside the breeding season, sometimes just circling around or following the predator as it moves away, or diving at it. It is usually birds of prey that receive this treatment, but other birds such as waders and Wood Pigeons, perhaps momentarily mistaken for a raptor, or species that might be feeding competitors, are often chased. Bats, another aerial insect-eater, are common targets of a Swallow's displeasure.

Roosting during the breeding season

The adults usually spend the night on or close by the nest, sometimes with the bill tucked into the wing. It is usually the female that roosts in the nest itself. When she has eggs or young nestlings, she covers them to keep them warm while the male perches nearby. Males, in contrast, often roost on wires, and perhaps sometimes in trees. When they have second broods, the males sometimes even leave their partners and roost communally. Fledglings usually return to their nest at night for another week or two, but they have to leave if their parents start another clutch. Even then they often roost in the same building as the nest, for as long as forty days, until they leave the area altogether. In some cases, a family of fledglings will roost with their mother in the nest until she starts laying again or even while she is incubating the second clutch; but in other cases, fledglings have been recorded roosting in trees outside the nest site. Any birds that have not bred during the season roost communally. Swallows sometimes also roost communally during cold weather at the start of the season, huddling together in buildings or in the nests of House Martins.

Breeding success

The number of pairs attempting a second brood is variable, and sometimes a few even have a third. In my study, eight out of ten pairs had two broods, but other studies have recorded as few as 35 per cent doing so. Third broods are most common in southern areas. In Florentino de Lope's study in Spain, 80 per cent of 351 pairs laid a second clutch and 13 per cent a third, whereas Karl-Heinz Loske found that among Swallows in central

Westphalia 74 per cent of 1169 pairs had a second brood and only 1 per cent a third. The percentage laying more than one clutch depends mainly on the weather and how early the Swallows started laying. Swallows usually breed quite successfully. Hatching success is typically high, at about 90 per cent or more (excluding complete clutch failures). On average, out of every ten eggs, seven to nine of them will hatch and produce a chick that is successfully reared to fledging. With two broods, a pair can generally produce six to eight young a year on average. The most successful pairs, with two large or even three broods, can rear more, sometimes even fourteen or fifteen. Losses are more often total nest failures than the loss of part of a clutch or brood. The few failures come about in a number of ways: starvation, parents dying or deserting, predators and parasites, nests falling down and destroying the clutch, or infertile eggs. In Derek McGinn and Hugh Clark's study in Scotland, for example, 76 per cent of eggs produced fledged young, 9 per cent were lost to predators (including humans), 7 per cent were lost because of a parent deserting, 1 per cent of losses were due to the death of an embryo or chick, and 7 per cent of eggs were infertile.

Bad weather is an important cause of losses. Eggs are sometimes deserted if bad weather makes it impossible for the female to incubate them, while chicks may starve if the weather is persistently cold and wet and the parents are unable to find enough food for them. In Anders Møller's study in Denmark, 29 per cent of nestlings that died starved, and Karl-Heinz Loske and Wolf Lederer recorded deaths of 16 and 20 per cent of first-brood nestlings in two wet summers in Germany. The temperature in the building where the nest is placed is not important – as many fledglings can be reared in cold barns as in warm stables – but that outside is crucial, as there are no flying insects to hunt in inclement weather. Losses from bad weather can occur on a large scale, but if there is a runt in the brood this one may suffer the most when food is scarce and, if weak from lack of food, may even be pushed out or crushed by its siblings. Too high a temperature is less of a problem than cold weather but there have been cases of nestlings dying from heatstroke.

Predation on eggs and nestlings is quite low, under 10 per cent usually being lost in this way. Few predators can get at the nest but cats, weasels, mice and rats are sometimes a problem and occasionally a corvid or owl destroys the contents of a nest or takes a sitting bird. Nests in exposed, easily accessible sites are most at risk. Other Swallows sometimes toss out eggs and kill young nestlings, too, as described in Chapter 5. In Møller's study, a third of nestling mortality was attributed to infanticide. Another 14 per cent was due to infestations by a mite, a subject on which I elaborate below.

Once out of the nest, fledglings face a number of predators such as Sparrowhawks that cash in on their inexperience at flying. Newly fledged birds, especially if they have left the nest early, may be incapable of flying far and end up on the ground, becoming vulnerable to terrestrial predators such as cats and dogs and even to scavengers. In one unusual case in North America, chipmunks were recorded eating recently fledged Swallows.

Families often roost near the nest once the young have fledged.

As well as predators, there are nest competitors to deal with. House Sparrows are a particular problem, as they will destroy the nest, destroy and remove eggs, and injure or even kill and remove young nestlings. Their depredations can be so severe as to make a pair of Swallows abandon its clutch or brood. In one study in North America, sparrows were thought to have reduced the reproductive rate of Swallows by 45 per cent over four years, being responsible for at least twenty deaths of nestlings and probably responsible for fifteen other deaths and 42 broken eggs in 24 out of 69 nests at the site. We do not know why House Sparrows behave like this; they could gain a nest site but do not always do so. Swallows will attack the sparrows, even though they may not succeed in keeping their nest.

As well as House Sparrows, other species such as House Martins, Robins, Wrens, Redstarts, Spotted Flycatchers and even mice will also occasionally use Swallow nests. Often they just take over an old, unused one, but disputes with the current owners are sometimes seen. Cuckoos (or cowbirds in North America) rarely lay an egg in a Swallow's nest, probably because of the difficulty of gaining access to one. This is especially so if the nest is close to a roof or overhang, where the gap above the nest is likely to be too small for a Cuckoo to squeeze in. Swallows themselves are sometimes highly aggressive in competition over nest sites, and they have been known to evict, for example, Spotted Flycatchers, Robins and a Blackbird. Sometimes they physically attack other birds: one is known to have drawn blood from a Black Redstart.

A number of animals live in the nests of Swallows, including parasites which can damage the health of adults and nestlings alike. Swallows in

Hilary Burn

Europe and North America have several kinds of parasites, including a blood-sucking blowfly, a group of specialized, flattened flies known as hippoboscids, bugs, mites, feather lice and fleas. In Britain, hippoboscid flies, although able to survive on Swallows, are usually found only in House Martins' nests, whereas on the Continent they are common inhabitants of Swallows' nests. Martin bugs and fleas are also Continental rather than British parasites of Swallows. Blowflies and mites are more serious threats to the nestlings, and at times these can be major pests. Other animals in the nest feed on these parasites; for example, booklice, bugs and pseudoscorpions feed on mites. Consumers of detritus and feathers such as some moth larvae may also be present.

Blowflies can be a significant cause of death among nestlings, especially those that are already weakened during periods of food scarcity. They live in the nests, and the larvae attach themselves to the skin between the toes, in the ears and nostrils, between emerging feathers, and around the neck and cloaca of the nestling, where they suck its blood. Some burrow into the skin and remain buried in the flesh of their victims. Their numbers build up during the breeding season, and infestations can reach high levels by the end of the summer, with sometimes more than thirty and occasionally up to 150 larvae attaching themselves to a single nestling.

Another important parasite of Swallows in Europe is a blood-sucking mite called the tropical fowl mite. Its natural history is well-known and Anders Møller has studied in detail how it affects Swallows. The mites secrete themselves into the lining of the Swallow's nest and underneath the bird's feathers, particularly on its head, where they are difficult to preen out. During the winter, more than 500 of these mites may bide their time in a single nest, waiting to clamber aboard the Swallows as soon as they return in the spring. The adult mites need two blood meals before they lay their eggs, and the young mites need blood, too. They grow quickly, becoming adult and ready to lay eggs of their own in a few days, so numbers build up rapidly during the summer. A badly infested nest at this time may harbour several thousand mites but the average is 50 – 60.

Not all nests are infested: in Denmark nearly half of nests with first clutches are, and about one in three nests with second clutches, although in a Spanish study the infestation level was higher at 60 – 100 per cent. Swallows returning in the spring deliberately avoid re-using nests containing a lot of mites. If mite-free nests are available, the Swallows choose these; if not, they will build a new one. The mites cannot travel between nests by themselves as the nests are spaced well apart; new nests are infected with mites already living on the birds (Swallows arrive at the breeding sites carrying parasites), and Swallows probably also pick them up when they visit nests and by direct contact with other birds. If the nest does contain mites when the first brood is being reared, the Swallows are then more likely to switch to another nest, refurbishing another old one or building a new one, for the second brood.

From egg to fledgling. The feathers cut through the skin at five to six days and the feather tips sprout at eight to ten days.

Not surprisingly, the nestlings suffer from the mites' feasts of blood. They are irritated by them and spend a lot more time preening themselves than do uninfested nestlings. More seriously, infested nestlings do not grow or survive so well as those that are free of mites. Anders Møller showed experimentally that nests containing mites are at a disadvantage. He first removed old nests and the mites inhabiting them from a breeding site during the autumn, so that the Swallows would build new nests, initially free of mites, the following spring. Some of the new nests he sprayed with pyrethrin to make sure they stayed free of mites; to others he added 50 mites; and others he just left alone. Chicks in nests infested with mites did not put on so much weight; they fledged a day or two prematurely, perhaps because of the irritations of the mites; and fewer of them survived than in nests that were free of parasites. They were at a disadvantage even when out of the nest because of their low weight and premature fledging, and were more likely to die during the difficult period when they had to learn to catch food for themselves.

Mites are a problem for the adults, too. The females' whole breeding success for the year is affected if mites are present in their nests. They annoy the female when she is incubating, forcing her to leave the eggs unattended more frequently. Consequently, in Møller's study, it took a day or so longer for females in mite-infested nests to incubate the clutch; they reared fewer offspring to independence, a week after fledging, from their first and second clutches; and fewer started a second clutch but if they did they took longer to do so and this second one was smaller than second clutches of females whose nests were free of mites. The effect of removing parasites (both mites and martin bugs) was even more marked in a study in Spain by Florentino de Lope and Anders Møller, at a site where females commonly have third broods: only 8 per cent of pairs left alone, with parasites in their nests, had a third brood, whereas 15 per cent had a third brood if their nest was fumigated to get rid of parasites once the first clutch had been laid, and 29 per cent did so if all their nests were fumigated. As with the Danish Swallows, the Spanish ones also took less time to initiate a second clutch and had heavier nestlings if they had nests without mites.

The breeding success of the adults is also affected by their own health, and mite-infested males may be less healthy. The blood-sucking habits of mites may weaken the birds, cause anaemia and transmit viral and other diseases. The more mites that males have during the breeding season, the less able they are to grow their tails longer at the next moult. Males troubled by parasites when they are rearing their first clutch are also poor songsters later in the season. These effects on tail length and singing ability damage the male's prospects for acquiring a mate. A male infested by parasites (particularly mites and lice) takes longer to acquire a mate and may fail to get one at all, even by cuckolding another male (see Chapter 5).

Individuals vary in their susceptibility to parasites and those that suffer badly in one year seem destined to suffer also in subsequent years. Their ability to cope with infestations is at least partly genetic. Møller showed this to be the case by cross-fostering newly hatched nestlings between nests to give Swallows mixed broods of their own and of fostered nestlings. He found that the numbers of mites infesting the nestlings depended on how badly infested their biological parents, and not their foster parents, were, suggesting that some birds are naturally more resistant to mite infestations than others, perhaps because of better immunological defences, and that they pass this resistance on to their offspring.

7

FEATHER CARE
AND MOULT

'Setting her compass–tremor tail–needles
She harpooned a wind
That wallowed in the ocean'
Ted Hughes

It is important for Swallows to spend some time keeping their feathers in good condition because they cannot fly efficiently if their feathers are out of place or damaged. In addition, dirt and parasites need to be removed. Swallows normally preen when perched, rearranging and repairing their feathers with the bill; they will also use their feet to scratch their heads, bringing the leg over the wing. They occasionally also scratch the head while in flight, in this case bringing the leg under the wing. Bathing is also done while on the wing. The bird dives down, dipping into the water, then emerging, flapping its wings and shaking its body to remove the water. As well as bathing in water, Swallows also bathe in dust or mud and have been seen bathing in the dew on a lawn and in the spray of a waterfall.

Sunbathing is also popular: Swallows often congregate on roofs, each with the back to the sun, wings and tail spread and feathers ruffled to expose the body to the warmth. Why Swallows sunbathe is not clear. They have been recorded basking on a metal roof in direct sunlight to the point of overheating, so keeping warm is clearly not the sole purpose of sunbathing. Several functions relating to feather care have been suggested:

Swallows bathe by dipping into the water while in flight.

It is essential for an aerial-feeding bird to keep its feathers in good shape.

the sun's rays may make parasites more mobile and easier to remove, they may soften the oil from the preening gland and so help the bird spread it over the feathers, or they may enhance the synthesis of Vitamin D.

Adult moult

Despite all the preening and bathing, by the end of the breeding season the feathers on a Swallow are decidedly worn, making the head and back look less glossy and the underparts whiter. To replace these feathers, Swallows undergo a single moult after breeding. Because Swallows feed in flight, moult has to be an extended, slow process. Hence those Swallows

99

migrating long distances, from Europe to southern Africa, defer the moult until they have reached the tropics. They do not have time for it between rearing their chicks and the onset of cold weather in the breeding areas which forces them south, and they could not fly and feed efficiently if they moulted during the migration. For the same reason, they cannot start the moult while still hunting food for nestlings or young fledglings. Some individuals do start replacing their inner primaries, tertials, wing-coverts or body feathers while still near the breeding grounds, but moult seems to be suspended while the birds are migrating. Primary moult, usually the innermost one or two, has been recorded in about 3 per cent of birds in Switzerland and Belgium, 7 per cent in Tien Shan, 10 per cent in Sweden and Germany, and 19 per cent further south in Spain. One Swiss bird had also started moulting its secondaries. One British adult bird started primary moult while still apparently breeding in mid-September.

As in other passerines, the primaries moult from the inner to the outer ones and the secondaries moult from the outer side towards the inner side, usually only one or two at a time in each wing. The first secondary is moulted at about the same time as the fifth primary and the last one when the last primary is moulted. The tertials moult in the sequence middle, inner and outer, starting at the same time as the first primary. The wing-coverts follow the moult of the main wing feathers but the secondary coverts are shed and grow together. The pairs of tail feathers are also shed from the centre ones outwards but the outer streamers may be shed before the penultimate pair and sometimes before the antepenultimate pair. The tail moult starts at about the time the fifth primary is shed. Because a Swallow has to maintain its ability to hunt insects efficiently at all times, wing and tail feathers are usually moulted symmetrically, but sometimes a feather is moulted on one side before its counterpart on the other. The body moult starts with the back and rump at about the same time as the first primary is moulted, continues with the breast and neck feathers and ends with the head feathers.

The moult starts with the first primary between mid-September and mid-November and can be well advanced by the time the birds wintering furthest south have arrived on the wintering grounds. It continues until the last primary is moulted in late January to late March, but is sometimes still incomplete by the time birds head north again. Some start to migrate while still moulting head feathers, tail feathers or primaries. The whole moult can take four-and-a-half to six-and-a-half months. Having only nine long primaries and a reduced tenth is presumably an advantage during moult as the whole process can be got over more quickly.

Even so, there is clearly not sufficient time for the whole moult to take place on the wintering grounds. The moult must be slow to allow the birds to continue hunting flying insects but the Swallows also need to return to their breeding grounds as soon as possible in the spring because an early start allows them to rear more offspring. They seem to compromise by continuing their moult after they have begun their northward journey. The streamers in particular take a long time to grow. Around Cape Town, more than 20 per cent of Swallows are still growing their tail feathers by the second week in April when the return north is well under way, and some Swallows in Europe have been found with tail feathers and the outer primaries still growing. A few Swallows even arrive back on the breeding grounds with growing tail feathers.

Swallows that breed in the southern parts of the range, such as those from north-western Africa, Libya, Iran, Iraq and parts of China, have less far to migrate than those from northern parts of the range, and they also start to breed earlier. Hence they have time to start their moult on the breeding grounds, finishing after their migration south: one female in Iraq started primary moult while still breeding. The races *transitiva* and *savignii*, as well as *rustica* from Afghanistan, Pakistan and India and *gutturalis* in the southern parts of its range, do not migrate or make only short movements away from the breeding sites. These moult early, even starting in late April, and finishing in September to November.

Juvenile moult

Immature birds moult up to six weeks later than adults in central Africa but only two or three weeks later than adults in southern Africa. Like adults, the vast majority of juveniles reared in northern regions do not start moulting until they reach the tropics but southern and resident birds start soon after fledging. Some do start moulting their body feathers in Europe, however, and continue to moult while on migration. Some of the innermost marginal and median coverts may also be moulted. Unlike adults, juveniles rarely start moulting their primaries while in Europe, but three juveniles have been recorded starting primary moult in Britain and four in northern Italy.

8

MOVEMENTS AND MORTALITY

'Thy nest's a bit of mine – thy little home
Set in the eaves.
When roses leave the wall, where wilt thou roam,
When summer leaves?'
Mary Coleridge

As summer degenerates into autumn, large numbers of Swallows, together with House Martins and Sand Martins, congregate on telephone wires, trees and buildings, ready to leave the cold winter to us and find warmer weather elsewhere. The exodus from Britain starts in August and is at its greatest in September and early October. At this time of year, Swallows may be seen in their hundreds or thousands. Eventually the autumn chill, the icy rain, the gales that wrench trees by their roots are too much: insect activity plummets and the gatherings of hirundines, so conspicuous one day, are gone the next. The onset of frosts at night will force all but a few stragglers to depart. These few hardy birds, however, may stay on in northern latitudes late into the autumn and winter. Further south, in southern Spain and Portugal and North Africa, Swallows overwinter regularly, and there are resident or partly resident populations in the eastern Mediterranean. In Britain the Swallow is one of the last migrants to leave and one or two are reported out of season in most winters. *The Atlas of Wintering Birds in Britain and Ireland* (Lack 1986) noted 147, although some records may have been of the same individuals. Most records were of late passage birds in November or early December in the south or south-eastern parts of the country, but two records in February in Lincolnshire and Norfolk may have involved birds overwintering. In late February, however, Swallows in Britain may be very early migrants returning home.

After breeding, Swallows roost communally, in groups ranging from a few birds to tens of thousands. They often gather in late summer and autumn at favourite roost sites such as reedbeds, willow scrub, tall grasses or fields of maize, some of the birds arriving from as far as 20 km away; less often they roost in trees, on cliffs or in Sand Martin burrows. Sometimes these roosts are shared with other birds such as Sand Martins and Pied Wagtails. In large roosts, the birds amass high in the air from several minutes to a few hours before roosting. At first they may fly rather aimlessly as individuals, but they soon form tight flocks and pass back and forth over the site in wheeling clouds, forming vast spirals and loops. As

Swallows roosting together in a reedbed.

the light fades, they plunge into the vegetation, first a few, then in great swirling waves of birds. They may be silent to begin with, but the last birds start to twitter as they drop and they may continue singing for several minutes once in the roost. As darkness settles, a few late birds may arrive and drop immediately into the roost. In reedbeds, the Swallows settle into the angles between leaves and stems, several birds per reed. There is some jostling and shifting of position, juveniles often having to make way for a pushful adult. In the morning, the birds usually leave en masse after sunrise. Nearly all the birds in these large roosts are juveniles, and in late autumn, when the adults have mostly left, roosts can be composed wholly of young birds. Communal roosts are not, however, just pre-migratory gatherings. They are used in midsummer, even by breeding Swallows who are still feeding nestlings, as well as by non-breeding adults and early-fledged youngsters.

During the day, non-breeding Swallows may move quite long distances. S. J. Ormerod, using data from the British Trust for Ornithology's ringing scheme, showed that Swallows in Britain move on average 20 – 30 km between roosts in one day. First-year birds wander in all directions to begin with, but during September and October they move more consistently towards the south-east. Movements to the north and west average 25 – 32 km over periods of up to ten days; but some are up to 270 km. Adults will also move northwards or westwards to roosts before migrating. These non-migratory movements may allow birds to assess future breeding and roosting sites (see below), but some may just be responses to local conditions which make some directions better for feeding, for example. The majority of Swallows at this time head south-east, but those from western Britain tend to stay on that side of the country and eastern birds on the eastern side. Swallows oriented to the south-east, and thus presumably on migration, move an average of 71 km, and up to 194 km, a day but they move further per day and seem less inclined to dawdle during September and October than in August. Ormerod found that over periods of up to ten days Swallows move an average of 47 km between roosts, only two or three times as far as they do if travelling between roosts within a single day, suggesting that they sometimes stop over for a few days at a site. This is not always the case, though: at some roost sites on the west coast, for example, the turnover of birds can be high.

Early views on hibernation and migration

To early naturalists, the mass disappearance of Swallows in the autumn and their reappearance in spring were well known but mysterious events. Some ancient Greeks considered the Swallow a bird of passage, flying to an unknown land for the winter, but Aristotle and Pliny considered that they must hide in crevices in rocks, remaining torpid, to escape the winter cold. Other naturalists thought they survived by diving under water and staying on the bottom, again torpid. This version of events seems to have taken root in the sixteenth century, when Olaus Magnus, Bishop of Uppsala in Sweden, reported fishermen pulling up nets full of Swallows, stiff and cold but which revived when taken into a warm room. A succession of such tales seemed to support this unlikely story and the subject was much debated particularly in the eighteenth and early nineteenth centuries, when these reports were frequent. The Abbé Spallanzani did carry out an experiment, putting Swallows in wicker cages under snow – the birds did not become torpid but died – but this negative evidence failed to sway current opinion. For people who did not know about migration, the idea that Swallows survived the winter hidden away in rock or mud was perhaps understandable, being based on observations of the way Swallows behaved as winter approached and in cold weather.

Swallows as well as some other species of swallow and martin, including the Sand Martin, White-backed Swallow and House Martin, are known to cluster together and enter a state of hypothermia in cold weather. Birds have been found sheltering together, sometimes on top of one another, in crevices in walls and cliffs, tree holes and holes in sand banks, inside buildings and in House Martin nests. Most instances of clustering are early in spring, late in autumn or over winter.

One recent report, for example, concerned eight Swallows in cold wet weather in May, before breeding had started, clustering in an old Swallow's nest at a site at the southern end of Lake Manitoba: the birds positioned themselves head first in the nest and struggled to go deeper into the cluster. In this case, one of the birds died despite being in the cluster, perhaps because its already meagre energy reserves were spent in trying to jostle its way into a good position. Exceptionally, severe weather during breeding also causes Swallows to behave in this way. Nils-Jarle Ytreberg recorded up to seven Swallows, including the nest-owners, huddling together for several hours in a nest containing eggs in wet, cold weather at a site in south-eastern Norway.

Falling into a state of temporary hypothermia enables a bird to save energy in particularly cold weather when food is scarce and when it has few or no fat reserves on which to draw. Experiments on Swallows show that they can drop their body temperature from 37.5 to about 30 – 35°C which allows them to use less energy. Clustering is also beneficial, enabling the birds to conserve their heat. A Swallow might survive a few days without food by dropping its body temperature and clustering but would die if the weather remained unfavourable for any longer. Indeed, many birds do not recover.

Although Swallows clearly cannot remain in this state for long, and certainly not over winter, people finding them in this state must have thought this evidence for a more prolonged hibernation. In addition, in the autumn Swallows commonly roost in large numbers in reedbeds. So it must have seemed reasonable that they spent the winter secreted in rocks or that they crept from the reeds down into the water and remained hidden at the bottom of ponds.

By the end of the eighteenth and the early nineteenth century, however, reports of Swallows seen at sea off the coast of Senegal and crossing the Mediterranean led naturalists to the view that they migrated from Europe to West Africa. One naturalist, Adanson, reported that Swallows appeared in Senegal only in winter and did not nest there, supporting the supposition that European birds migrate to Africa for the winter. There were also observations of Swallows far out to sea or flying out across the English Channel. The naturalist Gilbert White observed this himself and recorded that his brother in Andalusia had seen Swallows crossing the Straits in autumn and returning in spring; even so, Gilbert White was undecided about the fate of Swallows in winter and tended to favour the theory that they spent the winter under water. Thomas Forster,

Swallows often roost communally in reedbeds after breeding.

in his book *Observations of the Natural History of Swallows with a Collateral Statement of Facts Relative to their Migration and to their Brumal Torpidity*, published in 1808, weighed the evidence for and against the various theories and came down in favour of Swallows migrating.

It was not until the very end of the nineteenth century that people started ringing birds and so became able to trace their movements. Individual birds had been marked before. Caesarius von Heisterbach, prior of a German monastery, wrote in the thirteenth century of a man who supposedly fixed to a Swallow's foot a piece of parchment bearing the question 'Oh, swallow, where do you live in winter?', and in the following spring received the reply 'In Asia, in home of Petrus'. By tying threads dyed with water colours to the legs of Swallows, J. L. Frisch in Germany showed in the eighteenth century that the birds were unlikely to have spent the winter under water: the threads were still bright the following spring. Nowadays, thousands of Swallows are ringed each year, and well over a million have been ringed, each with an identification number, in Britain and Ireland alone. Thousands of these birds have been recovered, allowing ornithologists to build up a picture of where they spend the winter and which routes they take to get there and back.

Wintering areas

We now know that British (and Irish) Swallows migrate to South Africa for the winter, but the wintering sites within this part of Africa have not remained constant. Prior to the 1962/63 winter, they were recaught largely in the eastern regions of Transvaal, Natal, Orange Free State and eastern Cape Province, but since then they have expanded their range, moving into western Cape Province. This was probably due to a severe drought in the Transvaal that winter, making feeding conditions there poor for migrants. At the same time, vegetation and insects in the normally arid western Cape were flourishing as a result of recent heavy rains, providing a new and abundant crop of food for migrants abandoning the dry east.

Swallows from elsewhere in Europe migrate to different parts of Africa while those of the race *rustica* breeding in Asia winter mainly in the Indian subcontinent; some western Asian birds also winter in Africa. West European birds usually winter further to the west than east European ones, the east/west split occurring at about 15°E on the breeding grounds. Western and central European birds winter mainly in the western part of equatorial Africa from Liberia to the Congo between 10°N and 10°S and between 10°W and 26°E, whereas birds from eastern Europe, as far as 95°E, winter mainly farther east in central and East Africa between 22° and 34°E and also in eastern South Africa. Those from southern Europe also winter in the Congo basin. Swallows from any country, however, can end up in scattered areas of the wintering range; Swiss birds, for example, have been recovered in winter as far apart as Nigeria and Cape Province, and although many German birds winter in Zaire some winter in southern Ghana. Southern and south-western Africa have particularly mixed populations of west, central and east European birds, principally the former.

The Swallows from the northern parts of the range winter farthest south, leapfrogging more southerly breeders which are resident or move only as far as Central Africa. Two races, *transitiva* and *savignii*, mostly stay within their breeding range all year, although they do move out from the urban and village areas where they nest to swamps, lakes and cultivated fields. Some birds, especially juveniles, of the race *transitiva* do, however, make more extensive migrations, being recorded in Egypt, for example, and moving south, perhaps as far as East Africa.

The two Asian races also migrate south and winter in southern Asia and south-east Asia, although the most southerly populations are resident or migrate only short distances. The race *gutturalis* migrates as far as the Philippines, western Micronesia, the Sunda Islands, New Guinea and northern Australia and has been recorded wintering in south-east Africa.

The North American Swallow, race *erythrogaster*, winters in Central America south of Panama and, mostly, in northern and central parts of South America. Some winter as far south as Tierra del Fuego and some as far north as southern California and along the Gulf Coast.

Migration routes

In the autumn, European Swallows do not fly straight south to Africa. Central and western birds take a south-westerly or south-south-westerly route over France and the Iberian Peninsula to cross the western Mediterranean and western Sahara, and then change direction to reach central or southern Africa. British birds first head south-south-east,

The main migration routes of Swallows.

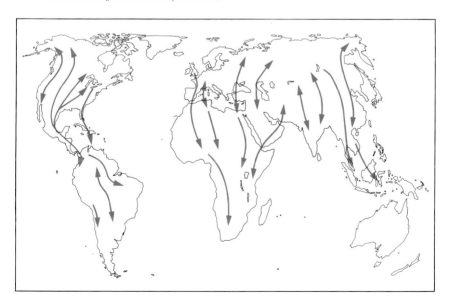

changing direction once in France to join the western flyline through western France and eastern Spain. Swallows from the north and from further east can also join the south-south-west route, but east European birds predominantly cross into Africa over the eastern end of the Mediterranean and the Middle East. The main passage across the Mediterranean is in mid-September to late October, with many birds arriving at their wintering grounds in November.

In contrast, the spring migration back to the breeding grounds is more direct: western and central European birds in northern Africa are recorded further to the east than in the autumn. Swallows start leaving the wintering grounds in February, many of them arriving at the Mediterranean and Middle East during the end of March and in April, and at their breeding grounds in late April and May.

The northward journey can be completed very quickly. There are records of Swallows flying 8500 km in 34 days, from Cape Town to Kutaisi in Georgia, and 12,000 km, also in 34 days, from Johannesburg to near Leninsk-Kuznetskiy in Russia. These birds must have flown at 250 and 350 km a day, respectively. About sixty days is probably a more common flight time, however, with an average distance flown of about 150 km a day. Swallows have been recorded flying at speeds up to 70 or 80 km per hour, but they do not fly continuously and directly when on migration, as they feed while en route and will follow valleys and coasts rather than making a beeline for home. In the autumn, the migration is also more leisurely than in the spring. Hence, both spring and autumn migrations take longer than the flight speed would suggest.

Swallows will form large flocks when flying on migration, but they usually fly in relatively small groups of a few tens of birds, which stay well spaced out, sometimes as a chain of single birds. The loose flocks facilitate feeding, giving each bird room to manoeuvre when pursuing an insect. Sometimes they fly in streams of birds, hundreds or thousands passing a point in an hour. They fly predominantly during the day, but some are recorded at night. At times, they break their journey to feed or to avoid an approaching storm and sometimes the flocks associate with other migrants, especially other hirundines but also, for example, swifts and bee-eaters.

We do not know exactly how Swallows find their way from their breeding sites to their wintering grounds and back again. Other long-

Swallows migrate in small, loose flocks.

distance migrants appear to use a combination of magnetic and sun or star compasses and it is likely that the Swallow does as well. Biologists have suggested that birds use a magnetic compass to perceive the angle of dip of the magnetic field, which varies with latitude. This allows them to determine the direction in which they need to fly. A sun compass may then be used to maintain that direction. Landmarks also probably help guide the bird once it is in an area it knows well.

At the breeding grounds, Swallows are clearly good at finding their nest site from some distance away. Some scientists have tested their homing ability by taking them several or many kilometres from the nest and seeing if they return to it. In these experiments the birds home quite well even when taken several hundreds of kilometres away. An early study in Germany showed that Swallows released in Athens and Madrid could fly home to Berlin (a distance of some 1800 km) in seven days, although not all birds made it back. The Ancient Romans used this homing ability to send messages about the outcomes of chariot races from Rome to Volterra, over 200 km away: they would take a Swallow to the race and tie a thread with the winner's colours on to its leg before releasing it; people waiting at the nest for it to return could then see who had won. During the Punic Wars in the third century BC, Swallows were taken from a besieged garrison so that the force relieving it could send them back to keep the garrison informed of their progress.

Coping with deserts and the weather

Crossing the Sahara and Sahel is a long and hazardous journey: more Swallows than any other bird species are reported dead in the desert. To cross the 1500 km or so can take at least two or three days, with little or no opportunity to stop and feed. To cope with this exertion, Swallows feed up beforehand, putting on up to a third more fat which they will use as fuel during the crossing. At an oasis in the northern part of the Sahara in spring Swallows weighed only 16 g, compared with 19 g at the south side of the desert, while in a cold spell in the oasis the Swallows' weights fell to less than 13 g and most were found dead. It is also likely that in autumn, while still in Britain, they fatten up when they can for the journey ahead. In a study of Swallows migrating through Wales, their average weight increased by 0.03 g per day between July and September, and by 2 – 3 g early in September when they start to migrate in earnest.

Wind, rain and low temperatures are all problems besetting Swallows on their way to and from Africa, particularly when they are crossing mountains such as the Alps; severe weather at such times can kill large numbers. Unlike many other migrants, particularly nocturnal ones, Swallows prefer to fly into the wind or in a cross-wind when on migration. This may be because they feed on the wing and so usually fly low down, at up to 100 m and often just a metre or so above the ground, where their insect prey are concentrated. If a Swallow were flying downwind and met a pocket of wind turbulence, which is most common at these low levels, the sudden drop in wind speed might make the bird stall. A head-wind is much safer to fly in. Wind speeds are also lower closer to the ground, facilitating hunting. Many other birds feed up at stop over sites and so can afford to fly at high altitudes, perhaps to avoid an unfavourable wind. Swallows, having to feed at lower levels while migrating, are also more restricted by the wind as to when they migrate. If the wind is unfavourable, they may temporarily halt their migration or occasionally even move in the reverse direction, although they do also occasionally fly at higher altitudes in a down-wind. Swallows probably undertake these reverse migrations in order to find better feeding sites or somewhere to roost overnight. In strong winds, they may have to seek out shelterbelts to find places where insects have accumulated. Wind is a particular problem for Swallows crossing stretches of sea over which they might be blown off course, further out to sea, where they are sometimes engulfed by waves.

Temperature is also an important factor in Swallow migration. Insects become scarce and localized at low temperatures, forcing Swallows to fly lower and perhaps diverting them from their course to search for good feeding sites. The movements of Swallows are usually more intense in warm weather, when the birds may also fly higher. This can be seen both during the day, as the air temperature rises, and through the season, as the Swallows' movements increase on warm days. Visual observations of migrating Swallows can, however, be misleading. In a cold spell, Swallows are conspicuous on migration because they have to keep to low altitudes to find enough food, whereas, when temperatures are high, they can feed up quickly and spend more time out of view at high altitudes. Rain and mist, like low temperatures, diminish the Swallows' food supply and affect their migratory movements, forcing them to feed lower down and to seek out certain sites such as lakes where insects are still available.

Swallows time their migration north in spring to coincide with rising temperatures and an increasing abundance of food. Unseasonally cold weather can therefore delay them. For example, in April 1974, the weather in North Africa was cold and hirundines were unable to feed – some were also killed by vehicles as they flew low – and they arrived late in Britain. Warm spring temperatures, on the other hand, as in late February and early March 1977, allow Swallows to move northwards quickly and they can arrive in Britain earlier than usual.

On the wintering grounds

Swallows are a dominant member of the bird community in Africa. With between 13 million and 33 million pairs breeding in Europe, some 100 – 300 million Swallows, together with 90 million or so House Martins and 300 – 400 million Sand Martins, may flood in to Africa from the Palearctic region each autumn. Once there, they face many potential feeding competitors: there are some nineteen other swallow species and nine swift species that breed in southern Africa, some at the same time as the Swallows are wintering there. As with the British species during the breeding season, however, (see Chapter 3), the different aerial-feeding birds segregate themselves, feeding in different sites and at different heights. Swallows in Africa feed low down over open ground and water, as they do when breeding. David Waugh found that their feeding sites overlap little with those of native swallows apart from the Grey-rumped and Wire-tailed Swallows and Brown-throated Sand Martins, but of these species only the Wire-tailed Swallow breeds at the same time as the Swallow is present, so competition for food is likely to be low.

A similar study of resident and migrant swallows in Malaysia by David Waugh and Chris Hails also showed little overlap between the different species. The Swallow feeds in similar places to the resident Pacific Swallow but at higher levels and often over the forest canopy, a feeding site avoided by the latter species. The type of food taken also differs, with Swallows feeding more on flying ants, especially just before the return migration, and less on flies than the Pacific Swallow, and generally taking smaller insects. In addition, although the resident swallow starts breeding while migrants are present, the peak period for rearing nestlings is at a time when most migrant Swallows have left.

A termite swarm is a good source of food for Swallows in Africa.

Swallows are nomadic on the wintering grounds but there is some evidence that individuals return to the same general area each winter. For example, in one study, of 60 birds ringed in the Transvaal and recaptured in subsequent years, 44 were recaught at the same place and thirteen within 40 km, and of eleven birds ringed in the Cape all were recaught within 30 km one or more years later. Swallows caught elsewhere have also turned up in the same area in subsequent winters.

Large flocks gather to roost on the wintering grounds, particularly when the Swallows are preparing to depart in the spring. Reedbeds are favoured sites for roosting, and maize fields are also often used in southern Africa. These roosts can be much larger than those on the breeding grounds, numbering thousands, even hundreds of thousands, of birds; roosts at Eldoret, Kenya, and near Tafo, Ghana, contain over a million, and two to three million Swallows congregate near Ndola, Zambia. Other birds, such as Sand Martins, sometimes roost with the Swallows. Elephant grass, bushes, trees, mangroves, sugar cane and other crops are also sometimes used. In addition, roosting Swallows have been recorded on the ground, on overhead wires and, in cold weather, in a barn. The resident races in North Africa gather in similar traditional winter roosting areas, although they sometimes also use nests in cold weather. In some areas, particularly in India and south-east Asia, as well as using more natural sites, Swallows often gather at night on overhead wires, buildings and ornamental trees in the well-lit town centres, sometimes with other swallows such as Pacific and Red-rumped Swallows and Sand Martins. One particularly large urban roost in central Bangkok contained 200,000 to 400,000 birds in the 1980s.

Swallows feeding over a wide area during the day will congregate at a large roost, flying in from several kilometres away. In Namibia, Swallows were recorded flying from 20 – 40 km into a roost, and in the urban Bangkok roost from up to 30 km. At large roosts, the majority of birds are juveniles, especially by the end of winter, when adults have started to head north. During the winter a Swallow may use more than one roost but long-term use of a single roost, for two birds at least 37 days, has been recorded. The behaviour of large numbers of Swallows at winter roosts, like that at post-breeding roosts on the breeding grounds, is spectacular. Great clouds of birds form shortly before sunset. They swirl high in the air for several minutes until dusk or shortly after when they drop into the reeds. As on the breeding grounds, the roosting Swallows may sing both before and after entering the roost. Karl-Heinz Loske noted that wintering Swallows tended to arrive at the roost closer to sunset than when on the breeding grounds, and formed tight flocks almost immediately rather than flying individually over the roosting site. He suggested that this was because wintering Swallows have a shorter day in which to feed, only some 12 hours, compared with 13 – 16 hours in central Europe, so they have less time to spare for apparently aimless pre-roosting activities.

The departure from the roost in the morning is equally dramatic. One observer, Kai Curry-Lindahl, described the scene at a reedbed roost containing an estimated 160,000 birds: 'The twittering and the rattling [of wings] increased to a crescendo. A few minutes later the reeds exploded into a cloud of swallows. They rose like helicopters straight up about ten meters or so, then spread out like an umbrella, ascended steeply, turned about in a half circle and then, without hesitation or breakfast, set out straight northwards.'

Returning to breed

Once back on the breeding grounds, those Swallows that have bred before return to last year's breeding site, often to the same nest and the same partner if he or she is still alive. Swallows are remarkably faithful to a breeding site and seem to move to a new nest site only if there were problems with the old one, and the previous breeding attempt failed, or if one of the partners has died. Eight or nine out of ten males will return to their previous nest site, many to the old nest while others use another nest nearby. In a French study, 96.6 per cent of adults that survived were faithful to the previous year's site, and in Oxfordshire 80 per cent of males were site-faithful. If they are widowed, males often still stay with the old nest and attract a new partner. Females are also faithful to a nest site, and often to a nest, but less so than males. They may, for example, move to a new site with a new partner if their previous partners fail to return. In Karl-Heinz Loske's study in central Westphalia, males that decided to move (7 per cent of them) moved only 233 m on average (and up to 750 m), whereas females (13 per cent) were prepared to move further away, 613 m on average (and up to 4600 m), from the previous year's nest. In his study in the Adirondacks, William Shields found that nearly half the males but only a quarter of the females used the same nest as in the previous year.

While partners are usually faithful to each other, divorces do occur both during and between breeding seasons. This is particularly likely if their last breeding attempt together was unsuccessful. After a breeding failure in the previous year, females usually change partners and nests, sometimes even nest sites, whereas after a successful breeding attempt they usually stay put. Males are much less likely to change nest sites after a breeding failure but if they do they do not move as far as females. In the Adirondacks study, males moved on average only 820 m if they had failed to rear young, but females moved 1200 m.

Returning to a familiar breeding site is a sensible strategy. The birds will already know where to find food and where to go to avoid predators. Some feeding sites will be best in sunny weather, others when it is windy or wet and cold, and some of these alternative feeding sites may be a long way from the nest site. So it will pay a Swallow to learn where they are just once in its first year of breeding, or even in its first autumn, rather than have to search for good places to feed each year. In addition, established partners can find each other easily and quickly and so avoid wasting time searching for and courting a new partner. Members of an established pair are also likely to get on well together and coordinate their activities, which may make their breeding attempt more successful.

There may be many reasons, however, why a change of nest, nest site or partner is desirable. Parasite populations, for example, can build up over

Swallows, and a Striped Swallow, roosting on wires in Kenya.

a season, so a shift to another nest may be required to avoid them (see Chapter 6). Birds of a pair can usually remain together for such a short move but if the partners do not get on, or their last breeding attempt failed because one of them did not contribute his or her share, or the nest site proved unsuitable because of lack of shelter from predators or the weather, one of the partners may want to move elsewhere and choose a new nest site or even a new partner. If this happens it is likely to be the female that goes, as it is easier for her to move to an unfamiliar site.

Males may be more reluctant to move because they benefit more than females from returning to a familiar nest site. This is because they have to compete among themselves to acquire a good site before they can attract a female. Once they have acquired such a site it may pay them to keep it in future years, even if their former partners decide to breed elsewhere. At a familiar site, males will have a nest that they can re-use, and if there are several they will know which is the safest and most sheltered. Knowing the neighbours could also be useful, as they are likely to be less aggressive to a familiar male than to a stranger and disputes over who owns what may be settled more quickly. Females gain similar advantages when they re-use a nest site but they do not have to fight with other females to get one; they can just choose a male and the site he has already acquired. So, if a female wants to find a better partner or nest site than she had the previous year, she can easily do so without getting involved in altercations with other birds at the new site.

One-year-old Swallows, in contrast to adults, return to the same general area but not the exact site where they were hatched. In a Spanish study, for example, fewer than one in a hundred fledglings returned to the same site. First-years return later than older birds, which take the best nest sites,

114

and so, as they cannot easily displace older birds, they are forced to move elsewhere. Most of these young birds return close to the natal site, 33 out of 42 to within 8 km in a British study and 49 out of 57 to within 15 km in a Danish study; but a few go much further, some of the birds in the British study moving up to 360 km for example. Occasionally, Swallows move quite long distances: one moved 410 km from Hessen to the former Czechoslovakia, and one from Belgium was found breeding in Morocco. Males are more faithful to the natal area than are females; in the central Westphalian study, males settled 740 m away on average, while females moved 2473 m.

Why females move further than males is not clear, but it may serve to reduce inbreeding. It does not, however, eliminate it because young birds still return to the same general area as the site where they hatched and about one in five birds nests on the same farm as its parents. There have been cases of females pairing with their sons and of a male pairing with his daughter. The immediate reason why males settle closer to the natal site may be that they get back before the females and it is up to them to choose a nest site and then try to attract mates. Young Swallows are known to disperse around their natal site before starting to migrate south and young males may take this opportunity to reconnoitre the local area, search for suitable breeding sites and then return to these familiar sites the following spring. Finding a good breeding site in an unfamiliar area may be too time-consuming in the spring, when time is at a premium. Young females are probably more interested in finding a good mate (see Chapter 5) and are less concerned with finding a nest site in a familiar area.

Juvenile and adult mortality

Many young Swallows fail to reach their first breeding season. Mortality varies, of course, from year to year and from site to site, depending on local conditions. On average, however, a pair of Swallows may rear six to eight chicks to fledging in a year. Recoveries of birds ringed as nestlings indicate that only one or two of these are likely to survive to the following breeding season. In several studies, the annual mortality of birds in their first year was 70 – 90 per cent, that is out of every 100 first-year birds only 10 – 30 will survive. Once over this hazardous year, Swallows survive a little better. Mortality of adults ranges from 43 to 73 per cent annually, with second-year birds tending to survive less well than three- or four-year-olds. Males and females have similar life expectancies, with females living marginally longer: in Britain, males may expect to live 1.59 years, and females 1.68 years. Swallows have been known to live for eleven or twelve years, and the oldest recorded was fifteen years and eleven months but extremely few are likely to reach their teens.

Mortality during the breeding season is generally low for adults compared with that at other times of the year. There are few predators of adults, but cats, owls, especially Barn Owls, and several birds of prey, especially Sparrowhawks, Merlins and Hobbies, take some, mainly young birds in the autumn while they are still inexperienced flyers. In a survey of

Hobbies are one of the few predators of Swallows.

the diet of the Hobby in central Europe, 30 per cent of the birds taken were Swallows. A few Swallows are killed when they mob predators (see Chapter 6). There are also a few records of other birds such as a Woodchat Shrike catching a Swallow. Odd records exist of unusual causes of death: for example, one low-flying Swallow was caught by a pike and another by a bullfrog, and a few have been killed by golfballs and entangled by brambles or loops of hair incorporated into the nest. There is little information on the numbers of birds colliding with power lines, windows and road traffic, but such incidents are occasionally reported despite the Swallow's expertise in the air. In a survey of British adult recoveries, 14 per cent of males and females recovered had hit a building, and 8 per cent of males and 5 per cent of females had been hit by a car or train, but these are probably biased, since dead Swallows near places frequented by people, such as buildings and roads, are in any case more likely to be found.

Swallows are one of the many species shot while on migration by hunters in the Mediterranean. Some countries, including France, Italy and Cyprus, have tried to reduce the numbers killed, but until recently shooting continued unrestricted in Malta. An estimated 160,000 to 430,000 swallows and martins have been killed annually in Malta, mostly just for target practice; often the shooters do not even bother to pick them up. They used to be taken for the pot or for sale in the markets, but now they are shot merely for 'fun'.

So far as we know, pollution generally has little impact on Swallows. A study of lead concentrations in Swallows nesting along highways in North America found no marked effect on their breeding success. The effect of modern pesticides on Swallows is not well known, apart from the indirect reduction in the birds' food supply, but accumulations of them may be harmful, especially in birds weakened by a period of bad weather. In the 1950s, DDT wiped out the Swallows breeding in an area of Israel (see Chapter 2). Swallows are sometimes the victims of major pollution incidents, such as the oil lakes which formed in Kuwait after Saddam Hussein had destroyed the country's oil wells during the Gulf War. Swallows were seen to dip down to the lakes as if trying to drink; some were enveloped in the oil and others were seen with tarred and sooty plumage.

The weather, through its effects on the food supply, plays an important role in the survival of Swallows, on the breeding grounds, on migration and on the wintering grounds. Most mortality of Swallows occurs during the winter and is related to the weather, since the birds need rain on the wintering grounds to produce a flush of insects (see Chapter 2). On a day-to-day level, the weather can affect how much fat the Swallow can put on, for example, when fattening up prior to migration. At the other extreme, in an extended spell of cold, wet weather when no or few insects will be active, Swallows and other hirundines, especially young birds, inexperienced in finding and catching insects, will die from exhaustion and starvation.

Sometimes the weather kills hirundines on a large scale. In Butte County, California at the end of April 1982, when the weather was unseasonally cold and wet, Barn, Cliff, Tree and Violet–green Swallows congregated in buildings to keep warm and over 100 were found dead. In Estonia, at the end of August 1952, strong winds and low temperatures caused mass deaths of hirundines; some Swallows flew into houses for warmth, while others became lethargic and settled on the roads, although some survived at least two days without food. Snow or prolonged rain is a particular hazard in some years when Swallows are crossing the Alps. In the autumns of 1931, 1936 and 1974, rescue operations were launched to take thousands of birds by plane or train over the mountains, although many other migrating birds died and many of those rescued were too weak to recover. In 1931, for example, a bird protection society in Vienna sent 89,000 birds by plane to Venice to be released. In October 1974 when depressions and cold northerly winds moved south-south-west over the North Sea, Europe had very cold weather, and many hirundines were caught out on migration; thousands came into south-east England from the Continent ahead of the fronts, and many entered houses and roosted on window ledges in an attempt to get shelter. In Africa, too, the weather can kill: tropical storms, torrential rain, sand storms, sudden cold spells and droughts all take their toll of wintering and migrating birds, and again this can be on a large scale. In November 1968, for example, cold wet weather in southern Africa was responsible for mass deaths of House Martins and Swallows, many of which had sought shelter in buildings.

9

SWALLOWS IN FOLKLORE

'The robin and the redbreast,
The martin and the swallow,
If ye touch one o' their eggs,
Bad luck will sure to follow.'
Anonymous

Humans have had a close relationship with Swallows for thousands of years. Because these birds originally built their nests on cliffs or in caves, they have readily taken to using the artificial 'rock faces' of our houses and outbuildings as nest sites, and they have thereby infiltrated our language, customs and folklore.

The Swallow is such a familiar bird that many things have been named after it. Terns are sometimes called sea-swallows because of their forked tails; several animals with forked tails are called swallow-tailed: for example, a hummingbird, a kite, a duck, a gull, a butterfly and a moth bear the name. Swallow wort is a herb the pods of which resemble a Swallow with outstretched wings; Greater Celandine, which flowers at the time Swallows return in spring, is also sometimes called Swallow wort. Various objects are also named after Swallows: a swallow-tailed coat has tapering skirts, and a swallow-tailed flag has two tapering points. A swallow dive is one in which the diver's arms are extended as in the outline of a gliding Swallow. The term 'swallow's nest' is applied to an object placed at a height, and especially to a battery of guns or company of shot. In a fortification, a swallow-tail is an outwork with two projections and a re-entrant angle between them; a barbed arrowhead is also called a swallowtail. Swallows are particularly symbols of speed and adorn British Rail's InterCity trains, as a sign (or perhaps more of a hope) that the journey will be swift.

Swallows are widely seen and celebrated as heralds of spring, returning warmth and fertility to the frozen winter landscape. Festivals and songs from Ancient Greece to Russia have heralded their return as the symbolic ending of the long cold winter. In Westphalia, it was the custom for the head of the family to open ceremoniously the doors of the barns and sheds on the day the Swallows returned to show them their quarters for that year. If the Swallows were not satisfied they were said to complain 'Last year, when I left,/All the sheds and barns were full,/Now, when I have returned/Everything has been spilt and destroyed and has rotted away'. Many customs have grown up around sighting the first Swallow of spring.

In the Tyrol, the observer must stand still and dig the earth beneath his left foot – the coal found there will cure a cold fever. In Westphalia, unmarried men should look under their feet: any hair they find there will be the colour of the hair of their future bride. In Bohemian folklore, unmarried men who see a single Swallow will marry within the year, but unmarried women will marry that year only if they see a pair of Swallows. In Spreewald, if you put your fist in your pocket for as long as the first Swallow is visible you will have lots of money all year.

The arrival of Swallows in Europe is often associated with particular Saints' Days or Easter, timed, it is said, to join in the celebrations: the feast of the Annunciation in Germany, Palm Sunday in Saxony, St Gregory's Day (12 March), St Joseph's Day (19 March), or St Benedict's Day (21 March) in Italy. The Chinese even used to set their calendar by them: the first official day of spring was the day the Swallows returned.

Because of their association with Easter, several Christian legends concern Swallows. In the Garden of Gethsemane, Swallows tried to lead astray those coming to take Christ. They are said to have removed the crown of thorns from Christ's head on the cross, staining their throat and forehead red in doing so. Other legends have them removing the nails from

---

A wire is a favourite perching site – Swallows have put our artefacts to their own use for thousands of years.

Christ's hands and feet, wiping blood from His wounds, consoling Him with their song or calling out 'He is dead, He is dead' to make the soldiers stop tormenting Him. A Swedish story tells that they called out to Christ 'hug svala hom', meaning 'fan him', commemorated in the Swedish name for a Swallow, *Svala*. A Swallow is also said to have brushed a fly from the eye of the Virgin Mary with its tail.

The Swallow is clearly seen as a virtuous bird, in God's favour and protected by him, in contrast to other species such as sparrows, which were imbued with evil. In a French legend, Magpies are accused of pricking Christ's feet with thorns while Swallows removed them: as a reward Swallows were allowed to nest in our homes, under our protection, while Magpies were banished to the tops of trees and endless persecution. In Westphalia, the Swallow is called 'Little Bird of our Lord' while in south Tyrol there is a saying that Swallows are consecrated to the Mother of God and therefore protected. One saying goes 'The Swallow and Swift are God's precious gift'. Christians do not always, however, have Swallows on their side: according to the Koran, Swallows attacked Christians who were besieging Mecca. Swallows also feature in more ancient religious stories. They are said to have been released by Noah as a sign of the start of a new era after the Flood, and to have reunited Adam and Eve after their expulsion from the Garden of Eden. In Austrian legend they helped God build the sky.

Swallows turn up in several other ancient legends. Athena became a Swallow in order to watch unseen as her suitors were destroyed, and Isis turned into a Swallow so she could flutter over the resting place of her murdered husband Osiris. In one Greek legend, Tereus married Procne, but fell in love with her sister, Philomena, raped her and cut out her tongue to prevent her talking; but she got word to Procne and the sisters ran away. When Tereus followed them they asked the gods for help; Philomena was turned into a Swallow and Procne into a Nightingale. The Swallow now twitters as if it has lost its tongue.

In eastern Europe and Asia, Swallows are traditionally the birds who brought fire from the gods to humans, losing their middle tail feathers in the process. In western Europe, the Swallow is said to have fetched the fire but the Wren or Robin took it and brought it to Earth. In one version of the legend, the Devil threw a firebrand at the thief, marking it red on its throat and forehead and burning out its tail feathers. In another, sparrows who were guarding the fire for the gods pecked out the Swallow's tail feathers. In Siberian legend, the tail feathers were lost when Tengri the Sky Being fired an arrow at the Swallow and hit the tail, whereas in Norse legend, they were hit by a thunderbolt thrown by Thor. In another legend, the Snake in Eden is said to have bitten the centre out of the Swallow's tail.

In Egypt, the Swallow was a 'sun bird', a messenger heralding the day and light and a symbol of the first piece of earth that rose up from the primeval waters. It is often depicted thus on tombs. It was also a minor deity in its own right, connected in particular with the region of the Theban necropolis, and was often mummified. In the 'Book of the Dead' there is a spell which enables the deceased to be transformed into a Swallow.

Such a virtuous bird is not surprisingly frequently regarded as a good omen. In Japan, gifts are offered to the household gods on the day the Swallows arrive to ensure fertility in the family. In many countries, and in many periods of history, a Swallow nesting in the house has brought good luck, and harming a Swallow or its nest bad luck. In Germany, Swallow nests were thought to protect buildings from lightning and fire. Disturbing a Swallow's nest would bring bad luck and would make the cows' milk bloody or dry up altogether; and the culprit's house would be struck by lightning or it would rain on his crops for a month. Bad luck would also ensue if a Swallow died in one's hand. Releasing a caged Swallow will bring good luck, or alternatively, remove bad luck, and cure misfortune such as infertility. In parts of Africa, Swallows are considered to be sent by the tribe's ancestors to comfort the living, and in Russian and Inuit mythology they are the spirits of dead children.

Swallows have also, however, been bad omens. Swallows building a nest on Cleopatra's flagship before the Battle of Actium were seen as a sign of impending disaster, as were Swallows nesting on the tent of Antiochus, the son of Pyrrhus, before he fought the Medes. The twittering or 'gossiping' of a Swallow at the siege of Helicarnassus foretold an act of disloyalty to Alexander the Great. In Yorkshire and Norfolk, Swallows in a chimney or gathering on the roof of a house foretold the death of a member of the household and (in Norfolk) they would take away his soul. In autumn they were said to gather on the roofs of churches to discuss who would die during the coming winter. A Swallow entering a room also foretold a death. In 1648, the story goes, the Rector of Stratton was drinking the health of King Charles I when a Swallow flew into the room, perched on his cup, and sipped his cider – a clear portent of the King's execution the following year. Another old saying is that a Swallow flying under your arm would paralyse you. In the Caucasus people believed that Swallows brought sickness with them in the spring, and in Germany, if you saw the first Swallow, you would get freckles. The Celts classed the Swallow along with the superficially similar Swift as devil birds, bringers of ill omen. In Ireland, if one removed a certain hair from your head, you would be damned for ever.

Traditional medicine has also made use of Swallows. They have been the basis of alleged cures for drunkenness and rabid dog bites (in ancient Assyria), kidney ailments (in China), angina and diphtheria (in Greece) and epilepsy and speech impediments (in Europe). The latter use may reflect a long-standing and widespread belief that like cures like: the Swallow with its stuttering song and fluttering flight was naturally thought of as the appropriate cure for stutterers and sufferers of fits. A seventeenth century cure for epilepsy involved pounding young Swallows to a pulp together with castor oil and white wine or white wine vinegar. The blood and the ashes of Swallows were thought to improve sight; the head, dried, to cure headaches; and the heart, eaten or worn around the neck, to improve memory and attractiveness. The heart, cooked in milk and carried on one's person, was also a guarantee that you would always keep everything that you possess. A widespread European legend, with many different versions, tells of a magic Swallow stone that can cure blindness, as well as epilepsy and slurred speech. Pliny thought that the stone could be found in the stomach of the eldest nestling in a brood of Swallows. Another version says that if you blind the nestlings, their mother will bring back the magic stone to cure them. Longfellow wrote of 'that wondrous stone, which the swallow/Brings from the shore of the sea to restore the sight of its fledglings'. In the Tyrol, the stones are thought to occur in nests used by Swallows for seven years in a row, and they could be found inside a nestling of the first brood cut open alive before the first full moon. In another version, there are three types of stone: a white one that will make you fairer; a red one that makes you more attractive to the one you love; and a green one that protects you against danger. In Mecklenburg, the stones are red, black or speckled and are found in the bodies, especially the livers, of nestlings; the red stone, worn under the left armpit in a purse of calf's leather, will improve memory and cure melancholy and headache. In 1586 a man accused of witchcraft, Hans Kröpelin, even claimed that a Swallow stone would make the wearer invisible.

Such tales as these are, of course, no longer widely believed and the threat of misfortune has not stopped modern farmers exterminating the Swallow's food supply and ripping out its hunting sites. Nevertheless, the Swallow is still much loved and heralded as a sign of the coming of summer. People still feel privileged to have a wild bird nesting with such apparent trust and confidence in and around their own homes. A countryside without Swallows twittering in the farmyard and flying with such grace and beauty over the fields would be as bleak as the winter banished by their arrival each spring.

Select Bibliography

Armstrong, E.A., *The Folklore of Birds*, Dover, New York, 1970

Ball, G.F., 'Functional incubation in male barn swallows', *Auk* 100 (1983), 998–1000

Boyd, A.W., 'Report on the Swallow enquiry, 1934', *British Birds* 29 (1935), 3–21

Brown, C.R., 'Vocalizations of barn and cliff swallows', *Southwestern Naturalist* 30 (1985), 325–33

Cramp, S. (ed.), *The Birds of the Western Palearctic, vol. 5*, Oxford University Press, Oxford, 1988

Crook, J.R., and Shields, W.M., 'Sexually selected infanticide by adult male barn swallows', *Animal Behaviour* 33 (1985), 754–61

Crook, J.R., and Shields, W.M., 'Non-parental nest attendance in the barn swallow (*Hirundo rustica*): helping or harassment?', *Animal Behaviour* 35 (1987), 991–1001

Curry-Lindahl, K., 'Roosts of Swallows (*Hirundo rustica*) and House Martins (*Delichon urbica*) during the migration in tropical Africa', *Ostrich* 34 (1963), 99–101

de Lope, F., 'La reproduction d'*Hirundo rustica* en Estremadure (Espagne)', *Alauda* 51 (1983), 81–91

Gibbons, D.W., Reid, J.B., and Chapman, R.A., *The New Atlas of Breeding Birds in Britain and Ireland: 1988–1991*, T. and A.D. Poyser, London, 1993

Jones, G., 'Parent–offspring resource allocation in Swallows during nestling rearing: an experimental study', *Ardea* 75 (1987), 145–68

Jones, G., 'Parental foraging ecology and feeding behaviour during nestling rearing in the Swallow', *Ardea* 75 (1987), 169–74

Jones, G., 'Time and energy constraints during incubation in free-living Swallows (*Hirundo rustica*): an experimental study using precision electronic balances', *Journal of Animal Ecology* 56 (1987), 229–45

Jones, G., 'Concurrent demands of parent and offspring Swallows *Hirundo rustica* in a variable feeding environment', *Ornis Scandinavica* 19 (1988), 145–52

Keith, S., Urban, E.K., and Fry, C.H., *The Birds of Africa, vol. 4*, Academic Press, London, 1992

Kozena, I., 'Dominance of items and diversity of the diet of young swallows (*Hirundo rustica*)', *Folia Zoologica* 29 (1980), 143–56

Lack, P., *Atlas of Wintering Birds in Britain and Ireland*, T. and A.D. Poyser, Calton, 1986

Loesche, P., Stoddard, P.K., Higgins, B.J., and Beecher, M.D., 'Signature versus perceptual adaptations for individual vocal recognition in swallows', *Behaviour* 118 (1991), 15–25

Loske, K.–H., 'Zur Brutbiologie der Rauchschwalbe (*Hirundo rustica*) in Mittelwestfalen', *Vogelwelt* 109 (1989), 59–82

Loske, K.–H., 'Nestlingsnahrung der Rauchschwalbe (*Hirundo rustica*) in Mittelwestfalen', *Die Vogelwarte* 36 (1992), 173–87

Loske, K.–H., and Lederer, W., 'Bestandsentwicklung und Fluktuationsrate von Weitstreckenziehern in Westfalen: Uferschwalbe (*Riparia riparia*), Rauchschwalbe (*Hirundo rustica*), Baumpieper (*Anthus trivialis*) und Grauschnäpper (*Muscicapa striata*)', *Charadrius* 23 (1987), 101–27

McGinn, D.B., and Clark, H., 'Some measurements of Swallow breeding biology in lowland Scotland', *Bird Study* 25 (1978), 109–18

Medvin, M.B., and Beecher, M.D., 'Parent–offspring recognition in the barn swallow', *Animal Behaviour* 34 (1986), 1627–39

Medvin, M.B., Beecher, M.D., and Andelman, S.J., 'Extra adults at the nest in Barn Swallows', *Condor* 89 (1987), 179–82

Medvin, M.B., Stoddard, P.K., and Beecher, M.D., 'Signals for parent–offspring recognition: a comparative analysis of the begging calls of cliff swallows and barn swallows', *Animal Behaviour* 45 (1993), 841–50

Møller, A.P., *Sexual Selection and the Barn Swallow*, Oxford University Press, Oxford, 1994

Ormerod, S.J., 'The influence of weather on the body mass of migrating Swallows *Hirundo rustica* in south Wales', *Ringing and Migration* 10 (1989), 65–74

Ormerod, S.J., 'Pre-migratory and migratory movements of Swallows *Hirundo rustica* in Britain and Ireland', *Bird Study* 38 (1991), 170–8

Peterjohn, B.G., and Sauer, J.R., 'North American Breeding Bird Survey Annual Summary 1990–1991', *Bird Populations* 1 (1993), 1–15

Shields, W.M., 'Factors affecting site fidelity in Adirondack Barn Swallows *Hirundo rustica*', *Auk* 101 (1984), 780–9

Shields, W.M., 'Barn swallow mobbing: self defence, collateral kin defence, group defence, or parental care?', *Animal Behaviour* 32 (1984), 132–48

Shields, W.M., and Crook, J.R., 'Barn Swallow coloniality: a net cost for group breeding in the Adirondacks', *Ecology* 68 (1987), 1373–86

Shields, W.M., Crook, J.R., Hebblethwaite, M.L., and Wiles-Ehmann, S.S., 'Ideal free coloniality in the swallows', in *The Ecology of Social Behavior* (ed. C.N. Slobodchikoff), pp. 189–228, Academic Press, San Diego, 1988

Smith, H.G., and Montgomerie, R., 'Sexual selection and the tail ornaments of North American barn swallows', *Behavioral Ecology and Sociobiology* 28 (1991), 195–201

Smith, H.G., and Montgomerie, R., 'Male incubation in barn swallows – the influence of nest temperature and sexual selection', *Condor* 94 (1992), 750–9

Smith, H.G., Montgomerie, R., Poldmaa, T., White, B.N., and Boag, P.T. 'DNA fingerprinting reveals relation between tail ornaments and cuckoldry in barn swallows, *Hirundo rustica*', *Behavioral Ecology* 2 (1991), 90–8

Tucker, G.M., Heath, M.F., Tomialojc, L., and Grimmett, R.F.A., BirdLife Conservation Series – *Birds in Europe: their Conservation Status*, BirdLife International, in prep.

Turner, A.K., and Rose, C., *Swallows and Martins of the World*, Christopher Helm, London, 1989

Waugh, D.W., *Predation Strategies of Aerial Feeding Birds*, PhD. thesis, University of Stirling, 1978

Waugh, D.W., and Hails, C.J., 'Foraging ecology of a tropical aerial feeding bird guild', *Ibis* 125 (1983), 200–17

Scientific Names

All species mentioned in the text are listed below with their scientific names.

Sparrowhawk *Accipiter nisus*
Kestrel *Falco tinnunculus*
Merlin *Falco columbarius*
Hobby *Falco subbuteo*
Peregrine *Falco peregrinus*
Grey Partridge *Perdix perdix*
Ruff *Philomachus pugnax*
Woodpigeon *Columba palumbus*
Cuckoo *Cuculus canorus*
Barn Owl *Tyto alba*
Little Owl *Athene noctua*
Swift *Apus apus*
Skylark *Alauda arvensis*
African River Martin *Pseudochelidon eurystomina*
White-eyed River Martin *Pseudochelidon sirintarae*
White-thighed Swallow *Neochelidon tibialis*
Tree Swallow *Tachycineta bicolor*
Violet-green Swallow *Tachycineta thalassina*
Purple Martin *Progne subis*
Brown-throated Sand Martin *Riparia paludicola*
Sand Martin (Bank Swallow) *Riparia riparia*
White-backed Swallow *Cheramoeca leucosternus*
Grey-rumped Swallow *Pseudhirundo griseopyga*

Crag Martin *Hirundo rupestris*
Swallow (Barn Swallow) *Hirundo rustica*
Red-chested Swallow *Hirundo lucida*
Angolan Swallow *Hirundo angolensis*
Pacific Swallow *Hirundo tahitica*
Welcome Swallow *Hirundo neoxena*
White-throated Swallow *Hirundo albigularis*
Ethiopian Swallow *Hirundo aethiopica*
Wire-tailed Swallow *Hirundo smithii*
Striped Swallow *Hirundo abyssinica*
Red-rumped Swallow *Hirundo daurica*
Cliff Swallow *Hirundo pyrrhonota*
Cave Swallow *Hirundo fluva*
House Martin *Delichon urbica*
Pied Wagtail *Motacilla alba*
Wren *Troglodytes troglodytes*
Robin *Erithacus rubecula*
Nightingale *Luscinia megarhynchos*
Black Redstart *Phoenicurus ochruros*
Redstart *Phoenicurus phoenicurus*
Blackbird *Turdus merula*
Spotted Flycatcher *Muscicapa striata*
Woodchat Shrike *Lanius senator*
Magpie *Pica pica*
Starling *Sturnus vulgaris*
House Sparrow *Passer domesticus*
Chaffinch *Fringilla coelebs*
Linnet *Acanthis cannabina*
Bullfinch *Pyrrhula pyrrhula*
Corn Bunting *Miliaria calandra*
Cowbird *Molothrus* spp.

INDEX